FINANCIAL INSTITUTIONS AND SERVICES

CREDIT SCORES

IMPACT AND ANALYSIS OF DIFFERENCES BETWEEN CONSUMER- AND CREDITOR-PURCHASED SCORES

FINANCIAL INSTITUTIONS AND SERVICES

Additional books in this series can be found on Nova's website under the Series tab.

Additional E-books in this series can be found on Nova's website under the E-book tab.

FINANCIAL INSTITUTIONS AND SERVICES

CREDIT SCORES

IMPACT AND ANALYSIS OF DIFFERENCES BETWEEN CONSUMER- AND CREDITOR-PURCHASED SCORES

PHILLIP B. ROGERS
EDITOR

New York

For permission to use material from this book please contact us:
Telephone 631-231-7269; Fax 631-231-8175
Web Site: http://www.novapublishers.com

Library of Congress Cataloging-in-Publication Data

ISBN: 978-1-62618-310-0

Published by Nova Science Publishers, Inc. † New York

CONTENTS

PREFACE

A credit score is a numerical summary of a consumer's apparent creditworthiness, based on the consumer's credit report, and reflects the relative likelihood that the consumer will default on a credit obligation. Credit scores can have a significant impact on a consumer's financial life. Lenders rely on scores extensively in decision making, including the initial decisions of whether to lend and what loan terms to offer, for most types of credit, including mortgages, auto loans, and credit cards. Credit scores also influence the marketing offers that consumers receive, such as offers for credit cards. A good credit score can mean access to a wide range of credit products at the better rates available in the market, while a bad credit score can lead to greatly reduced access to credit and much higher borrowing costs. This book provides context for understanding the credit reporting industry as a whole, important industry players, and the complexity of the credit scoring process.

Chapter 1 - A credit score is a numerical summary of a consumer's apparent creditworthiness, based on the consumer's credit report, and reflects the relative likelihood that the consumer will default on a credit obligation. Credit scores can have a significant impact on a consumer's financial life. Lenders rely on scores extensively in decision making, including the initial decisions of whether to lend and what loan terms to offer, for most types of credit, including mortgages, auto loans, and credit cards. Credit scores also influence the marketing offers that consumers receive, such as offers for credit cards. Further, credit scores affect account-management decisions, like raising or lowering credit limits or changing interest rates. A good credit score can mean access to a wide range of credit products at the better rates available in the market, while a bad credit score can lead to greatly reduced access to credit and much higher borrowing costs.

Lenders use credit scores that are produced by many different scoring models. The most widely used scores are the "FICO scores" sold by FICO (the brand used to identify the Fair Isaac Corporation). There are a number of FICO score models in use by lenders, and many other credit score models besides the FICO scores. Consumers can also purchase a wide range of credit scores. Some scores sold to consumers are used by lenders, but others, referred to as "educational scores," are either not used by lenders at all or are used only infrequently. It is important to note that many of the credit scores sold to lenders are not offered for sale to consumers. The Dodd-Frank Wall Street Reform and Consumer Protection Act requires the Consumer Financial Protection Bureau (CFPB) to "conduct a study on the nature, range, and size of variations between the credit scores sold to creditors and those sold to consumers by consumer reporting agencies (CRAs) that compile and maintain files on consumers on a nationwide basis,… and whether such variations disadvantage consumers." Consumers can purchase scores from the CRAs in several ways. They can purchase scores when they request copies of their credit reports directly from the CRAs, or with their annual free credit file disclosure available through annualcreditreport.com. The CRAs or their marketing partners also sell scores as part of "credit monitoring" or "identify theft" products.

When a consumer purchases a score from a CRA, it is likely that the credit score that the consumer receives will not be the same score as that purchased and used by a lender to whom the consumer applies for a loan. This could occur if the score the consumer purchased is an educational score that is not used by lenders, but differences between the score a consumer buys and the score a lender buys can occur for other reasons as well. Since so many scores are in use in the marketplace, it could also be the case that the particular lender to which the consumer applies uses a different scoring model than the one purchased by the consumer, or that the CRA from which the consumer obtains a score is not the same CRA that the lender uses to obtain scores, or that the underlying data in the consumer's credit report changes significantly between the time the consumer purchases a score and the time the lender obtains a score for that consumer. It is also possible that a consumer and a lender could access different reports from the CRA, if they were to use different identifying information about the consumer. Any of these differences could lead to differences between the credit score a consumer sees and the credit score a lender uses to assess that consumer. A consumer, unaware of the variety of credit scores available in the marketplace, may purchase a score believing it to be his or her "true" (or only) credit score, when in fact there is no such single score. Believing he or she had purchased a FICO score may lead to dissatisfaction upon learning otherwise. The consumer may be frustrated to learn that they cannot know exactly how a creditor will view them. But the most significant adverse impact on a consumer from score differences would likely occur if the credit scores the consumer buys give a substantially different impression of his or her credit risk than credit scores that a lender would use. This could occur if there are substantial differences between the scores sold to consumers and those sold to lenders. In this scenario, some consumers may settle for less favorable terms or may forego applying for credit if the scores they purchase lead them to believe they will be viewed as poor credit risks, although the scores received by lenders would imply otherwise. Alternatively, a consumer who incorrectly expects to be considered a good credit risk may apply for loans for which he or she could not qualify, leading to disappointment, wasted effort, and unnecessary inquiries on a credit report, which could depress his or her score further. This report provides context for understanding these issues by describing the industry as a whole, important industry players, and the complexity of the credit scoring process. It then examines the ways credit scores are obtained and used, and discusses how the differences between the scores provided to creditors and those provided to consumers could disadvantage consumers. Additionally, the report details a substantial data collection and analysis project being carried out by the CFPB that will help characterize the differences between the scores provided to consumers and those provided to creditors.

Chapter 2 - When consumers purchase their credit scores from one of the major nationwide consumer reporting agencies (CRAs), they often receive scores that are not generated by the scoring models use to generate scores sold to lenders.

The Dodd-Frank Wall Street Reform and Consumer Protection Act directed the Consumer Financial Protection Bureau (CFPB) to compare credit scores sold to creditors and those sold to consumers by nationwide CRAs and determine whether differences between those scores disadvantage consumers. CFPB analyzed credit scores from 200,000 credit files from each of the three major nationwide CRAs: TransUnion, Equifax, and Experian. The study yielded the following results:

- The CFPB found that for a majority of consumers the scores produced by different scoring models provided similar information about the relative creditworthiness of the consumers. That is, if a consumer had a good score from one scoring model the consumer likely had a good score on another model. For a substantial minority, however, different scoring models gave meaningfully different results.

- Correlations across the results of scoring models were high, generally over .90 (out of a possible one). Correlations were stronger among the models for consumers with scores below the median than for consumers with scores above the median.
- To determine if score variations would lead to meaningful differences between the consumers' and lenders' assessment of credit quality, the study divided scores into four credit-quality categories. The study found that different scoring models would place consumers in the same credit-quality category 73-80% of the time. Different scoring models would place consumers in credit-quality categories that are off by one category 19-24% of the time. And from 1% to 3% of consumers would be placed in categories that were two or more categories apart.
- The study looked at results within several demographic subgroups. Different scores did not appear to treat different groups of consumers systematically differently than other scoring models. The study found less variation among scores for younger consumers and consumers who live in lower-income or high-minority population ZIP codes than for older consumers or consumers in higher- income or lower-minority population ZIP codes. This is likely driven by differences in the median scores of these different categories of consumers.
- Consumers cannot know ahead of time whether the scores they purchase will closely track or vary moderately or significantly from a score sold to creditors. Thus, consumers should not rely on credit scores they purchase exclusively as a guide to how creditors will view their credit quality.
- Firms that sell scores to consumers should make consumers aware that the scores consumers purchase could vary, sometimes substantially, from the scores used by creditors.

In: Credit Scores
Editor: Phillip B. Rogers
ISBN: 978-1-62618-310-0

Chapter 1

THE IMPACT OF DIFFERENCES BETWEEN CONSUMER- AND CREDITOR-PURCHASED CREDIT SCORES*

Consumer Financial Protection Bureau

EXECUTIVE SUMMARY

A credit score is a numerical summary of a consumer's apparent creditworthiness, based on the consumer's credit report, and reflects the relative likelihood that the consumer will default on a credit obligation. Credit scores can have a significant impact on a consumer's financial life. Lenders rely on scores extensively in decision making, including the initial decisions of whether to lend and what loan terms to offer, for most types of credit, including mortgages, auto loans, and credit cards. Credit scores also influence the marketing offers that consumers receive, such as offers for credit cards. Further, credit scores affect account-management decisions, like raising or lowering credit limits or changing interest rates. A good credit score can mean access to a wide range of credit products at the better rates available in the market, while a bad credit score can lead to greatly reduced access to credit and much higher borrowing costs.

* This is an edited, reformatted and augmented version of the Consumer Financial Protection Bureau, dated July 19, 2011.

Lenders use credit scores that are produced by many different scoring models. The most widely used scores are the "FICO scores" sold by FICO (the brand used to identify the Fair Isaac Corporation). There are a number of FICO score models in use by lenders, and many other credit score models besides the FICO scores. Consumers can also purchase a wide range of credit scores. Some scores sold to consumers are used by lenders, but others, referred to as "educational scores," are either not used by lenders at all or are used only infrequently. It is important to note that many of the credit scores sold to lenders are not offered for sale to consumers. The Dodd-Frank Wall Street Reform and Consumer Protection Act requires the Consumer Financial Protection Bureau (CFPB) to "conduct a study on the nature, range, and size of variations between the credit scores sold to creditors and those sold to consumers by consumer reporting agencies (CRAs) that compile and maintain files on consumers on a nationwide basis,... and whether such variations disadvantage consumers." Consumers can purchase scores from the CRAs in several ways. They can purchase scores when they request copies of their credit reports directly from the CRAs, or with their annual free credit file disclosure available through annualcreditreport.com. The CRAs or their marketing partners also sell scores as part of "credit monitoring" or "identify theft" products.

When a consumer purchases a score from a CRA, it is likely that the credit score that the consumer receives will not be the same score as that purchased and used by a lender to whom the consumer applies for a loan. This could occur if the score the consumer purchased is an educational score that is not used by lenders, but differences between the score a consumer buys and the score a lender buys can occur for other reasons as well. Since so many scores are in use in the marketplace, it could also be the case that the particular lender to which the consumer applies uses a different scoring model than the one purchased by the consumer, or that the CRA from which the consumer obtains a score is not the same CRA that the lender uses to obtain scores, or that the underlying data in the consumer's credit report changes significantly between the time the consumer purchases a score and the time the lender obtains a score for that consumer. It is also possible that a consumer and a lender could access different reports from the CRA, if they were to use different identifying information about the consumer. Any of these differences could lead to differences between the credit score a consumer sees and the credit score a lender uses to assess that consumer. A consumer, unaware of the variety of credit scores available in the marketplace, may purchase a score believing it to be his or her "true" (or only) credit score, when in fact there is no such single score. Believing he or she had purchased a FICO score may lead to dissatisfaction upon learning otherwise. The consumer may be frustrated to learn that they cannot know exactly how a creditor will view them. But the most significant adverse impact on a consumer from score differences would likely occur if the credit scores the consumer buys give a substantially different impression of his or her credit risk than credit scores that a lender would use. This could occur if there are substantial differences between the scores sold to consumers and those sold to lenders. In this scenario, some consumers may settle for less favorable terms or may forego applying for credit if the scores they purchase lead them to believe they will be viewed as poor credit risks, although the scores received by lenders would imply otherwise. Alternatively, a consumer who incorrectly expects to be considered a good credit risk may apply for loans for which he or she could not qualify, leading to disappointment, wasted effort, and unnecessary inquiries on a credit report, which could depress his or her score further. This report provides context for understanding these issues by describing the industry as a whole, important industry players, and the complexity of the credit scoring process. It then examines the ways credit scores are obtained and used, and discusses how the differences between the scores provided to creditors and those provided to consumers could disadvantage consumers. Additionally, the report details a substantial data collection and analysis project being carried out by the CFPB that will help characterize the differences between the scores provided to consumers and those provided to creditors.

I. Credit Reporting and Credit Scoring

In order to evaluate how credit scores affect consumers it is necessary to understand how the underlying data is compiled, how scores are created, and how they are used by lenders. This section provides background information on credit reporting and credit scoring. Subsequent sections describe the market for scores sold to lenders and how lenders use scores, and the market for scores sold to consumers.

A. Consumer Reporting Agencies and Credit Reports

Consumer reporting agencies are companies that gather, organize, standardize, and disseminate consumer information, especially credit-related information. In mandating this study, the Dodd- Frank Act refers specifically to scores provided by "consumer reporting agencies that compile and maintain files on consumers on a nationwide basis,"[1] also called "nationwide CRAs." The three nationwide CRAs are TransUnion, Equifax, and Experian.[2] For the purposes of this study, these three firms are referred to as "the CRAs."

Most consumers with a history of using credit products will have a file at each of the three CRAs. The CRAs collect, among other information, credit account information including the amount of a loan, the credit limit on a credit card, the balance on a credit card or other loan, and the payment status of the account; items sent for collection; and public records, such as judgments and bankruptcies.[3] The CRAs compile the information into files about individual consumers. The CRAs also track requests, or "inquiries," for a consumer's credit data, and records of those requests are maintained in the consumer's file.[4] Consumer files are used to produce reports that the CRAs provide to creditors, insurance companies, potential employers, and other users. These reports are formally called "consumer reports" but are often referred to as "credit reports," which is how they will be referred to throughout this report.[5] The activities of CRAs, creditors, and others that provide data to the CRAs (often referred to as "data furnishers"), and users of credit reports are governed by the Fair Credit Reporting Act (FCRA), which is concerned with, among other things, the "accuracy and fairness of credit reporting."[6]

Each of the three CRAs may have somewhat different information in a particular consumer's file for a variety of reasons: not all data furnishers provide data to all CRAs; data furnishers may provide information to the different CRAs on different schedules; and a CRA will only have records of inquiries that it, not the other CRAs, received. In addition, the process of matching consumer information received from a data furnisher to consumer files is a complex one, and consumers' address and name changes make tracking particularly difficult.[7] These matching issues also may lead to differences among the consumer's files at the CRAs, as each CRA has its own matching process and logic.[8]

B. Credit Scores

Credit reports can contain a great deal of detailed information, especially for consumers with extensive credit histories. Credit scores take that information and turn it into a single numerical summary.[9] FICO developed the first credit scores for use by lenders in the 1950s. Since then, and especially since the 1980s, versions of the "FICO score" and various other scoring models have been adopted for use by credit card issuers, auto lenders, mortgage companies, and other types of lenders. Credit scores permit lenders to standardize, centralize, and automate underwriting processes.

The CRAs generate scores from the data in the credit files in their records and provide those scores to creditors. Other credit scoring entities, such as some large lenders, use data from one or more of the three CRAs, sometimes in combination with other data the lender itself may collect, to generate their own credit scores. Credit scores "rank order" consumers by predicted credit risk. That is, a score shows whether a consumer is more or less likely to repay a debt *relative* to other consumers. The absolute probability that a consumer will not pay a debt will depend on the type of credit product, broader economic conditions, and a wide range of other factors.

To generate a score, the CRA or the lender applies a mathematical algorithm, or "scoring model," to the information in the credit report being used.[10] As part of this process, it is first necessary to create summaries of various aspects of the information in the report, because detailed information about the consumer's credit accounts cannot be fed directly into a scoring model. For example, records of individual accounts are used to determine characteristics such as the age of the oldest credit account, the number of accounts 60 days past due or worse in the last two years, or the ratio of total balances on credit cards to total credit limits. The summary variables that are generated from the raw data are referred to variously as "credit attributes," "credit variables," or "roll-ups." Each of the CRAs has hundreds of attributes that have been created at various times for various purposes, but a typical scoring algorithm uses far fewer.

The primary factors that affect credit scores include:

- payment history, including late payments and collection items;
- balances, available credit, and the percentage of existing credit lines being utilized;
- negative public records such as bankruptcy, judgments, and liens;
- length of the credit history and the mix of credit types; and
- evidence of taking on new debt, such as new accounts or inquiries.

When credit scores are designed and sold to predict payment behavior on a wide range of credit products, they are referred to as "generic" scores. When they are designed to predict performance on a specific type of credit, such as automobile loans, they are referred to as "industry" scores. Some lenders, especially larger lenders, receive credit reports from a CRA and calculate scores themselves using models developed to predict the performance of their own population of customers. These are called "custom" scores.

There are numerous generic and industry scoring models in use at the three CRAs. Some were developed by the CRAs themselves, while others were developed by third-party scoring companies, such as FICO. In addition, there are numerous custom scores in use by various individual lenders. A credit scoring model that is better at predicting future payment behavior by consumers conveys a competitive advantage to a lender, and therefore a score developer, so credit scoring models are highly valuable, closely guarded intellectual property.

II. Credit Scores in the Marketplace

Credit scores are ubiquitous in the consumer credit marketplace. Lenders use them to determine not only whether to grant credit but also what amount of credit to provide and on what terms. Because CRAs can deliver credit reports and scores almost instantly upon request, the use of credit scores and automated underwriting make possible the granting of "instant" credit in venues where obtaining credit could be an important part of a consumer's purchase decision, such as at an auto dealer or a department store. Incorporating the use of credit scores enabled the government-sponsored enterprises, Fannie Mae and Freddie Mac, to introduce automated underwriting systems that enabled loan officers and other mortgage originators to streamline the mortgage underwriting process.

Credit scores also facilitate "risk-based pricing" by lenders. When lenders use risk-based pricing, they offer applicants with poor credit histories less favorable terms than they offer to consumers with better credit histories. Risk based pricing allows some consumers with poor credit histories to obtain credit, but at higher cost than consumers with good credit histories. Various terms have proliferated – like prime, near-prime, sub-prime, and deep sub-prime – that represent groups of consumers whose credit scores occupy different points or "bands" along a spectrum of good to poor credit risk. In particular, FICO score "bands" within its range of 300 to 850 have become widely used shorthand to define groups of consumers by their risk characteristics. The particular numerical bands vary from lender to lender and over time; for example, "prime" borrowers who present low risks of default have at various times referred to consumers whose FICO scores were at or above 620 or 680.

A. Types of Credit Scores

1. FICO Scores

As described above, FICO developed the first credit scores in the 1950s, and the FICO scores are still the most widely used generic scoring models. One industry observer estimates that FICO had over 90 percent of the market share in 2010 of scores sold to firms for use in credit-related decisions.[11]

There are numerous FICO scoring models. Because of differences in the data at the three CRAs, FICO develops unique generic scoring models for use at each of the three CRAs.[12] There are also several different generations of generic FICO scores in use, and FICO develops industry models for credit cards, mortgages, and auto loans.

All scoring models FICO creates are built to generate scores that fall in the range 300 to 850. Different FICO scoring models, however, may produce minimum or maximum scores slightly above 300 or slightly below 850.

Fannie Mae and Freddie Mac, the government-sponsored enterprises that purchase and securitize a large portion of mortgages for the secondary mortgage market, require the use of FICO scores in the underwriting of mortgages that they will purchase.[13] The Federal Housing Administration (FHA) has also required that mortgage lenders wishing to originate FHA-insured loans must use FICO scores.[14] These requirements mean that, in the current mortgage market, most mortgages are underwritten using FICO scores.

2. Consumer Reporting Agency Scores

The CRAs each have their own proprietary generic scoring models. These scoring models were originally developed to predict performance on credit obligations, but are currently sold primarily as "educational scores" for consumers. [15] Examples of the proprietary generic scores sold by the CRAs are the following:

- Equifax: "Equifax Credit Score." Produces scores in the range 280-850.[16]
- Experian: "Experian Plus Score." Produces scores in the range 330-830.[17]

- TransUnion: "TransRisk New Account Score." Produces scores in the range 300-850.[18] This scoring model was developed to predict performance on new credit accounts, unlike the standard FICO score or the VantageScore, which were developed to predict risk on both new and existing accounts.

The CRAs also build custom scores for individual clients on a contract basis.

3. VantageScore

VantageScore LLC is a score development company established as a joint venture of the three CRAs. The VantageScore models generate generic scores. A basic difference between VantageScore's models and the FICO models is that for each generation of VantageScore, the model is the same at each of the three CRAs. VantageScore builds its models using development databases that combine data from all three CRAs. If all data about a consumer were the same at each of the three CRAs, the VantageScore for that consumer would be the same no matter which CRA's credit report was used to provide the data. However, the scores may vary in the event that the information at the CRAs differs.[19]

There are currently two VantageScore models in use. The original VantageScore was released in March 2006; an update of the VantageScore model, VantageScore 2.0, became available for use in January 2011.[20] The VantageScore models produce scores on the range 501-990.

B. Uses of Scores

Though the primary use of credit scores in credit markets is to make an initial lending decision, they are used throughout the credit life cycle.

1. Marketing

Scores are used in the pre-screening process to determine what credit offers, especially credit card offers, to send to consumers.

2. Origination

Scores are used at the origination stage for all types of consumer credit. Scores are one factor used to determine whether to offer an applicant a mortgage, which specific types of mortgages the borrower can receive, and what interest rate, points, and fees the borrower will pay. Similarly, for auto loans, scores affect whether an applicant can obtain a loan, the maximum amount of the loan, the interest rate, and whether a co-signer will be required to qualify for the loan. For credit cards, scores can affect not only the decision of whether to offer credit, but also the interest rate, the credit limit, and the product features – such as fee or no-fee, rewards or no-rewards – that a consumer will be offered.

3. Account Maintenance or Account Review

Credit card issuers periodically review their customers' credit reports and scores to decide whether to raise or lower credit limits and interest rates and whether to make special offers such as balance transfers. Other lenders also may use scores in their credit management processes, or to evaluate whether to cross-sell new products to existing customers.

4. Valuations of Loan Portfolios

Credit scores on individual borrowers are used by owners and buyers of loan portfolios, or of securities backed by such portfolios, and by rating agencies, to predict the likelihood and timing of the borrowers' loan repayments, and the future cash flows that are used to assess the portfolios' values.

III. Consumer Credit Score Marketplace

Consumers can purchase credit scores in at least two ways. They can buy them as an add-on when obtaining a credit report from a CRA or certain other vendors, or they can receive them as part of a "credit monitoring" service. Some of the scores consumers can purchase in this way are used widely by creditors; others are not. In any case, if a consumer buys a score, it is quite likely that any particular lender that consumer approaches for a loan will use a different score, given the diversity of scores in use in the market.

In light of the important role of credit scores in consumer credit markets, there is a great deal of interest on the part of consumers in obtaining their credit reports and credit scores. The market for providing credit reports and scores has grown in recent years to more than $1 billion in revenue, and sales to consumers make up roughly a quarter of the U.S. revenues of the CRAs and their affiliates.[21]

In addition to consumer credit score purchases, there are several circumstances in which a lender is required to provide a consumer with a score, as discussed further below. In these cases, the score comes from the lender using the score, and the score the consumer receives will likely be a score that was used by the lender.

A. Consumer Purchases of Credit Scores

The FCRA entitles consumers to request and receive disclosures of their credit reports from a CRA at any time for a fee or, for free in certain circumstances, such as if they are victims of identity theft.[22] In addition, the FCRA entitles consumers to obtain one free disclosure of their credit report in any given 12-month period from each of the three CRAs through a "central source." In compliance with the latter requirement, the CRAs have established a jointly-owned limited liability corporation, Central Source, which manages a toll-free number, mailing address, and website (annualcreditreport.com) through which consumers can receive their credit report disclosures. The Consumer Data Industry Association, a trade group representing the CRAs, estimates that approximately 30 million free credit reports are delivered annually through the central source. This number represents approximately 15.9 million individual consumers, as many consumers obtain reports from more than one CRA each year through the central source. Fourteen percent of one CRA's credit report deliveries through the central source resulted in the purchase of a credit score by a consumer.[23] If this rate is similar at the other two CRAs, an estimated 4.2 million score disclosures are made annually through the central source.

When consumers request their credit reports directly from a CRA or through the central source, the FCRA dictates that they have the option to purchase a credit score calculated using the credit report.[24] In this context the consumer receives credit scores based on scoring models chosen by the individual CRA. The scores sold by the CRAs to consumers through this channel may be educational scores.

In addition to these mandated credit score sales channels, consumers can purchase scores through services typically identified as "credit monitoring" or "identity theft protection." Many of the scores sold through these channels are educational scores. Affiliates of each of the three CRAs, as well as the CRAs' direct marketing partners, offer ongoing access to credit reports and accompanying credit scores through these programs. The CRA affiliates are able to obtain credit reports about consumers from the other CRAs for this purpose, so a consumer can obtain reports from all three companies through a single enrollment. Consumers generally obtain these services on a subscription basis by enrolling at the service provider's web site or via outbound telemarketing.[25] As an industry, credit monitoring services have grown rapidly with a reported 26 million active subscribers in 2010.[26] Consumers generally learn about the services from direct advertising on television and the Internet and through communications from lenders, such as credit card issuers.

The CRAs market, accept enrollments and payments for, and deliver services through their own company-branded consumer websites (Equifax.com, Experian.com, and TransUnion.com), as well as other specialty-purpose sites.[27] Some of the CRAs also sell the services at wholesale through third party marketing companies, which brand and resell the services separately.[28] Some companies sell credit monitoring services through financial institutions, which offer the services to their credit card and banking customers, in some cases under the financial institutions' brand.

When a consumer obtains a credit report and accompanying credit score directly from a CRA, through the central source, or through a credit monitoring service, the particular credit score he or she receives depends on which scoring model the CRA marketing affiliate – or in some cases, the marketing partner – has chosen to make available to consumers. As all three of the nationwide CRAs have their own business units that provide analytic and credit score development services to lenders, it is not surprising that each CRA would consider providing scores based on their internally developed algorithms to consumers, thereby avoiding paying a licensing fee with each score sale to a third party such as the FICO. All three CRAs do provide scores based on their own scoring models or the scoring model developed by their three-way joint venture VantageScore. Equifax also offers for sale a FICO score with an Equifax credit report.

The landscape of service brands and websites has evolved rapidly and continues to change. Table 1 summarizes the current landscape of credit scores provided through some of the three CRAs' affiliated credit monitoring services and through services offered by major third-party marketers of credit monitoring services.

It is useful to note that FICO scores are currently available for purchase with respect to the credit reports of only two of the three CRAs: Equifax and TransUnion. At present, myfico.com is the only channel through which a consumer can directly purchase a FICO score on a TransUnion credit report, and until recently, myfico.com and Equifax.com were the only two channels through which consumers could purchase a FICO score on an Equifax credit report. One bank recently announced it was offering its customers their FICO scores based on Equifax credit files for a monthly fee.[29] FICO does not have a licensing agreement with Experian for providing FICO scores to consumers, so there is no service through which a consumer can purchase an Experian credit report with an accompanying FICO score.[30]

Table 1. Credit Monitoring Providers and Services

Monitoring Service Provider	Brand(s) and Web Address(es)	Consumer Credit Score(s) Offered
Equifax	www.equifax.com	Equifax Credit Score FICO Score
Experian	www.experian.com www.freecreditscore.com www.freecreditreport.com www.familysecure.com	Experian PLUS Score
TransUnion	www.transunion.com www.truecredit.com	VantageScore (previously, the TransRisk Score)
Affinion	www.privacyguard.com www.identitysecure.com (markets through websites of various financial institutions)	CreditXpert Score
Intersections	(private label websites for various financial institutions)	CreditXpert Score
Vertrue	www.privacymatters.com www.freescore.com www.creditdiagnosis.com www.creditadapter.com	VantageScore
FICO	www.myfico.com	FICO Scores

The CreditXpert score that is sold through several services was developed by CreditXpert specifically for sale to consumers, rather than to creditors.[31] It was not developed to predict performance on credit obligations, but rather to provide information about how a consumer will be scored by other models in the marketplace. CreditXpert also offers a suite of services that allow a consumer, or a lender working with a consumer to help the consumer qualify for a particular loan, to evaluate how different changes to the consumer's credit report would affect the consumer's credit score.

B. Mandatory Provision of Credit Scores by Lenders

The FCRA, as amended by the Dodd-Frank Act, requires lenders to provide consumers with credit scores in certain circumstances.[32] These generally include when: (1) a lender provides credit based, in whole or in part, on a credit report or score using risk-based pricing; (2) a consumer applies for a mortgage loan; and (3) a lender denies or revokes credit, changes the terms of an existing credit arrangement, or refuses to grant credit in substantially the amount or on substantially the terms requested (adverse action). These instances of mandatory lender-provided scores provide a useful context for assessing the impact of the credit scores that consumers purchase.

1. Receiving a Credit Score in Connection with Risk-Based Pricing

Lenders often use the information in a credit report as a factor to grant materially less favorable loan terms to a consumer than the most favorable material terms available to a substantial proportion of consumers from or through that lender. [33] Lenders who engage in risk-based pricing to provide credit based on a credit report generally are required to provide either (1) a "risk-based pricing notice" – which, after July 21, 2011, will include a credit score – or, as an alternative, (2) a "credit score disclosure" to all applicants.[34] The specific requirements for each type of disclosure vary according to the type of credit. A credit score disclosure includes the consumer's scores as well as information on how the consumer's credit score compares with that of other consumers.

2. Receiving a Credit Score When Obtaining a Mortgage

Home mortgage originators are generally required to provide applicants with a credit score distributed by a CRA used "in connection with an application initiated by or sought by a consumer for a closed end loan or the establishment of an open end loan" secured by residential real property, along with an explanatory notice.[35] Mortgage applicants may also receive a risk-based pricing notice.[36]

3. Receiving a Credit Score on an Adverse Action Notice

Under amendments to the FCRA made by the Dodd-Frank Act that will become effective on July 21, 2011, when an applicant is denied a loan, or otherwise is subject to an adverse action, and the lender bases that adverse action in whole or in part on any information contained in a consumer report, the lender is generally required to provide an adverse action notice that includes, among other disclosures, a numerical credit score used by the lender in taking the adverse action.[37]

Many of these credit score disclosure requirements represent recent amendments to the FCRA and related implementing regulations. Prior to January 2011, the only context in which lenders would have been required to provide a credit score to a consumer would have been when the consumer applied for a mortgage.[38] At the beginning of this year, the Board of Governors of the Federal Reserve System and the Federal Trade Commission finalized rules requiring lenders engaging in risk- based pricing to provide certain disclosures to consumers. At the lender's option, those disclosures could include a credit score, and in certain cases, a distribution of credit scores or the key factors that adversely affected the consumer; however, they did not require them.[39] After the changes made by the Dodd-Frank Act go into effect on July 21, 2011, lenders who engage in risk-based pricing based on a credit report or score must generally provide credit scores to consumers to whom they extend credit, and they will also have to provide credit scores to consumers when taking an adverse action against them.[40] Consumers will then begin to see and receive many more credit scores than they had been exposed to previously.

IV. Analysis of Potential Harms to Consumers

When a consumer purchases a credit score from a CRA, he or she will often receive a score that will not be the same score used by a lender to evaluate the consumer's creditworthiness. The complexities of the consumer reporting and credit scoring environment, the variety of scores in use in the marketplace, and the choices by the CRAs of which scores to sell to consumers provide some explanation for why this is the case. This section discusses possible adverse effects on consumers that could result from these differences, as well as a substantial data collection and analysis project being carried out by the CFPB that will help characterize the differences between the scores provided to consumers and those provided to creditors.

A. Potential Adverse Effects on Consumers

How consumers could be negatively affected if the scores they obtain are different than the scores used by prospective lenders depends on why consumers obtain scores and what they do with the scores they purchase. It also depends on what they believe they are obtaining and what they believe they learn from scores.

There is little research available about why consumers purchase credit scores. The focus of the advertising from score marketers is on (1) planning ahead for a large purchase, such as a home or automobile,[41] (2) improving consumers' credit scores, similar to the way individuals are encouraged to improve their fitness,[42] (3) monitoring of consumers' financial health generally, and (4) alerting consumers to possible identity theft.

There is also little research about consumer understanding of credit scores. Earlier this year, VantageScore and the Consumer Federation of America released the results of a survey of a representative sample of 1,000 Americans who were asked a number of questions about credit scores.[43] Almost half of the consumers surveyed did not know that a credit score is designed to indicate the risk of not repaying a loan. However, 71 percent of those surveyed said that they knew that most Americans have more than one generic credit score. Nearly 60 percent were confused about the scale of credit scores,[44] and only 25 percent of those surveyed knew that scores are "available from numerous web-based sources, not just from FICO or the three main credit bureaus."[45]

A consumer, unaware of the variety of credit scores available in the marketplace, may purchase a score believing it to be his or her "true" (or only) credit score, when in fact there is no such single score. The scarcity of public educational tools to inform consumers of the differences among credit scores, the large combined market share and brand recognition of FICO scores, and the marketing practices of some credit score sellers, may all perpetuate such confusion. In these circumstances, the consumer would have spent money on a score or subscribed to a credit monitoring service that he or she otherwise might not have purchased. Believing he or she purchased a FICO score may lead to dissatisfaction upon learning otherwise. Most importantly, the consumer may be frustrated to learn that they cannot know exactly how a creditor will view them.

The most substantial harm would likely result if, after purchasing a score, a consumer has a different impression of his or her creditworthiness than a lender would. This could occur because the consumer obtains a different score than the lender, or because the consumer simply misunderstands the significance of the score he or she obtains. As discussed below, in a follow-up study, the CFPB will quantify the differences between the credit scores available to consumers and those used by creditors. This follow-up study will provide more information about the potential for harm; for now, this discussion focuses on the possible types of harm.

If a consumer obtains a score that makes the consumer believe that he or she is a better credit risk than lenders would determine, based on the scores lenders see, the consumer may apply for loans for which they will not be approved. This will waste the consumer's time and, possibly, money. For example, the consumer may pay application fees for loans for which he does not qualify. It also has the potential to hurt the consumer's credit score, as credit applications result in credit report inquiries, which generally have a negative effect on credit scores.

If, on the other hand, the consumer obtains a score that makes him or her believe he or she is a worse credit risk than lenders would believe, the consumer may apply to lenders that offer less favorable terms. The consumer may apply for or accept loans with higher interest rates, for lower amounts, or with otherwise worse terms than other loans for which the consumer would qualify. A lender may not have an incentive to clear up the consumer's confusion. In addition, consumers who believe they are worse credit risks than they are may not seek out credit that they would benefit from and could qualify for, believing they would be denied or that the credit would be too costly.

Given the numerous scores in use by creditors, it is difficult for consumers to know exactly how they will be evaluated. Consumers might not know the actual score that a lender will use, or may not be able to obtain that score. This will not cause problems for consumers if the scores that they purchase give them very similar information as those used by creditors. Consumers may be harmed, however, if the scores they purchase give them different information. The potential extent of this harm will be assessed directly as part of the subsequent analysis described below.

B. Data Analysis

The CFPB will obtain a substantial database in order to analyze further the nature, range, and size of variations between the credit scores sold to creditors and those sold to consumers by the CRAs. The results of this analysis will shed light on whether the potential harms described above could be occurring, and to what degree. The data will consist of credit reports and scores for 200,000 individuals from each of the three nationwide CRAs. Those data will allow for the assessment of credit score variations in detail both for the overall population of consumers and for sub- populations.

1. CRA Data

Each of the CRAs has agreed to construct a random sample of 200,000 consumer reports from its database, in consultation with CFPB staff.[46] For each consumer report in each sample, the CRA will prepare a record containing the entire credit report for the individual, a set of the most commonly used credit attributes, and credit scores generated for each credit report. The credit scores will include the scores the CRA sells to consumers and several of the scores that are most widely sold to lenders by the CRA.[47] For each of the credit scores provided, the CRA will also provide the trade-name of the score and the four most important key factors that adversely affect the credit score of the consumer in the model used. These key factors are required to be delivered with credit scores provided with consumer credit file disclosures under the Fair Credit Reporting Act.[48]

The CRA will remove all personally identifiable information, such as name, Social Security number or date of birth, from each record, and assign a new "Study ID" to each record. The CFPB will not receive any personally identifiable information. The Study ID will be generated specifically for the purpose of providing the data to the CFPB and will not identify the consumer in any way. The purpose of the Study ID will be to allow, if necessary, CFPB staff to identify particular records to the CRA, discuss and resolve any apparent problems in the database, for example.

These databases should allow a thorough analysis of differences between scores sold to consumers and scores sold to creditors. The detailed credit history information will make it possible to explore whether differences in scores across models are more likely to affect consumers with different credit history features, and the databases will be large enough for analyses of even narrowly defined sub- samples.

2. Analysis

The purpose of the data analysis will be to determine with greater precision and understanding the nature, range, and size of variations between the credit scores most frequently sold to creditors and those most frequently sold to consumers. For ease of exposition, in this section the credit scores sold to consumers will be referred to as "consumer scores" and the credit scores sold to creditors will be referred to as "creditor scores." There are a number of ways to characterize how similar consumer scores are to creditor scores, as identified below, each of which may be useful in further analyzing the issues discussed in this report. As a general matter, when comparing scores generated by two different scoring models, one can either compare the actual numerical scores or compare the consumer's relative ranking in the credit risk distribution indicated by the score.

a) Absolute Comparisons

Absolute comparisons – comparisons of the actual numerical scores – are most useful for comparing scoring models that use the same range, such as scores from two models that both use the FICO score range of roughly 300 to 850. Absolute comparisons would also be appropriate to evaluate how misinformed consumers would be if they compared two scores generated by models that use different ranges but the consumers did not know that fact – for example, in the case of a consumer comparing a FICO score with a VantageScore. The VantageScore range is 501 to 990.

The absolute score differences can be evaluated in a number of ways, for example by reviewing the:

- average of the absolute value of the score differences;
- share of consumers whose two scores both fall in the same range of numerical scores; and
- share of consumers for whom the consumer score is greater than a creditor score by a certain amount, and, similarly, the share of consumers for whom the consumer score is less than the creditor score by a certain amount.

b) Relative Comparisons

Relative comparisons could be made by first converting scores into measures of the relative credit- worthiness represented by the scores, for example determining each consumer's percentile rank in the score distribution for each score. This would be most useful when comparing scores that come from scoring models that use different ranges, such as FICO scores and VantageScores. This type of comparison is most relevant when consumers understand what the score they obtain indicates about their relative riskiness.

Relative comparisons can be evaluated in ways analogous to the evaluation of absolute comparisons, for example, by reviewing the:

- average of the absolute value of the differences in ranking in the score distributions;
- share of consumers whose scores fall in the same percentile range of scores; and

- share of consumers for whom the rank of the consumer score is greater than the rank of the creditor score by a certain amount, and, similarly, the share of consumers for whom the consumer score is less than the creditor score by a certain amount.

c) Comparisons within Score Sub-Groups

Any of the absolute or relative score comparisons described above can be made for sub-groups defined by score ranges: for example, the average absolute value of the difference between the consumer scores and the creditor scores for consumers whose consumer score is in the bottom ten percent of scores. Similarly the share of consumers whose consumer and creditor scores fell in a particular score range, or percentile range, could be calculated: for example, the share of consumers whose consumer scores are in the bottom 10 percent of consumer scores, as well as the bottom 10 percent of creditor scores, or the 10 percent to 20 percent range of creditor scores.

d) Comparisons within Groups Defined by Credit History Characteristics

Because the CFPB is obtaining detailed credit report data, comparisons will also be possible for sub- samples that are defined by particular credit history characteristics. For example, consumers with limited credit histories, or "thin files," can be analyzed separately, to determine if they are more or less likely to have large differences between their consumer and creditor scores; and consumers with particularly "clean" histories can be analyzed separately.

CONCLUSION

Credit reports and scores play a central role in lenders' decisions about whether and under what terms to extend credit to consumers. This fact explains, in part, why the business of providing credit reports and scores to consumers has grown to more than $1 billion in revenue annually, accounting for roughly one-fourth of the U.S. revenues of the nationwide CRAs and their affiliates.

There are numerous credit scores that could be calculated for a consumer, using different scoring models or data from different CRAs, and each of those scores will change over time as the information in a consumer's credit report evolves. Given this complexity, it is unlikely that a consumer will often be able to know the exact score that a particular lender will use to evaluate them.

This report explains why this complexity arises and the various ways that consumers obtain scores, and identifies ways in which differences between the scores consumers purchase and the scores that lenders receive could lead to potential consumer harm. In subsequent analysis the CFPB will obtain and analyze data that shed further light on differences in scores and the significance of related concerns.

APPENDIX. CREDIT SCORE MODEL DEVELOPMENT

New scoring models are constantly being developed, and each scoring model is unique. Firms develop new scoring models for a variety of business reasons, but the primary purpose is to produce a model that does a better job of predicting consumer behavior, as this can convey a competitive advantage on the lender using the model. Specific reasons why a firm may develop a new model include to:

- update the model, in case the relationships among particular credit attributes and credit performance have changed over time;
- incorporate new data elements that may be available;
- implement technological improvements in scoring methodologies; and
- build a model that predicts consumer behavior on a particular credit product, such as car loans or credit cards, or in particular geographic markets, or for a particular segment of prospective customers.

To build a generic credit scoring model, developers start with a sample of consumers whose credit reports can be observed for a period of time in the files of a CRA.[49] The developers collect the credit reports for those customers for two points in time, or "snapshots," from archives maintained by the CRA. The period between the two snapshots is typically about two years, and is referred to as the "performance period." The fundamental approach to model development is to construct a statistical model that uses the data available in the first snapshot to make predictions about consumers' payment behavior during the performance period, which is captured in the second snapshot.[50] The resulting statistical model is used to construct a scoring model to predict the behavior of other consumers.

Developers must make a number of decisions when they are building a credit scoring model, all of which can create variations among credit scoring models. They must decide how to characterize payment behaviors as "good" or "bad." A common approach is to call any payment that becomes 90 or more days past due "bad," but there are different approaches that will produce different scoring models.[51] These "good" and "bad" payment behaviors are the outcomes that the score developers attempt to predict. Model developers also must decide how to construct credit attributes.

Score developers use the first snapshot of data to construct numerous credit attributes, like those described previously, that summarize the consumers' credit reports. These attributes are then used as predictors of "good" and "bad" outcomes. Using various statistical techniques, the developers identify credit attributes that are associated with "good" payment behavior, as well as credit attributes that are associated with "bad" payment behavior. These identified attributes are used to construct a statistical model of future payment behavior, the details of which will vary among developers due to the different decisions made during model development.

The final step in building a credit scoring model is to use the statistical model of payment behavior to construct a specific scoring algorithm that uses consumers' credit attributes as inputs to produce credit scores that fall in a certain numerical range, or scale. If the scoring model being developed is intended to replace an existing model with an established score range, the new model will likely be constructed to produce scores on the same scale. However, different score developers may well choose to develop scores that use entirely different scales. Scoring models differ from each other depending on their purpose, construction, and data source. Specific causes of scoring model variances include differences in:

- underlying data used to develop the score, for example, because they were obtained from different CRAs or from different time periods;
- type of credit product for which the model was built;
- numerical range of credit scores produced;
- definitions of "good" and "bad" credit behavior; and,
- credit attributes used in the model, due to the numerous ways to summarize information in a credit report into credit attributes.

End Notes

[1] Dodd-Frank Wall Street Reform and Consumer Protection Act, Pub. L. No. 111-203, § 1078 (2010) (hereinafter the "Dodd-Frank Act"):

STUDY AND REPORT ON CREDIT SCORES.

(a) STUDY.—The Bureau shall conduct a study on the nature, range, and size of variations between the credit scores sold to creditors and those sold to consumers by consumer reporting agencies that compile and maintain files on consumers on a nationwide basis (as defined in section 603(p) of the Fair Credit Reporting Act; 15 U.S.C. 1681a(p)), and whether such variations disadvantage consumers.

(b) REPORT TO CONGRESS.—The Bureau shall submit a report to Congress on the results of the study conducted under subsection (a) not later than 1 year after the date of enactment of this Act.

[2] Federal Trade Commission, 75 Fed. Reg. 9726, at n.2 (Mar. 3, 2010) (online at www.ftc.gov/os/2010/02/100223facta.pdf).

[3] For a detailed summary of the data compiled by the CRAs, see Robert B. Avery, et. al., An Overview of Consumer Data and Credit Reporting, Federal Reserve Bulletin, at 47-73 (Feb. 2003) (online at www.federalreserve.gov/pubs/bulletin/2003/0203lead.pdf).

[4] Requests from the consumer for copies of the report, as well as requests for the purposes of marketing firm offers of credit, are not included in consumer reports that are provided to creditors and other users and are not factored into consumers' credit scores. Such requests are typically referred to as "soft" inquiries.

[5] This report will use the term "credit report" to refer to both the consumer reports, 15 U.S.C. § 1681a(d), purchased by users, such as lenders, and to the documents obtained or purchased by consumers who wish to see the information contained in a consumer report that a lender might obtain. The Fair Credit Reporting Act refers to the latter documents as "disclosures to consumers." 15 U.S.C. § 1681g.

[6] 15 U.S.C. § 1681a.

[7] For example, a consumer who has recently married, moved, and changed her name may have two reports about her at a CRA that have not yet been combined. Depending on the information the consumer and lender use to request the score or report, they may obtain credit scores that differ based on their use of different reports.

[8] Federal Trade Commission, Report to Congress under Sections 318 and 319 of the Fair and Accurate Credit Transactions Act of 2003, at 35-55 (Dec. 2004) (online at www.ftc.gov/reports/facta/041209factarpt.pdf).

[9] There are also lending-decision models that incorporate data beyond that on the credit report, such as income data from an application. These types of models may also generate a numerical score, but this is different from a "credit score" as the term is used here. There are also other users of credit reports besides lenders, and some of these users employ scoring models. Some employers and landlords use credit report information when making hiring and rental decisions, and many automobile and homeowners insurance companies use credit-based insurance scores in underwriting and rating, except where prohibited by state law. While these uses of credit reports and scores have serious implications for consumers, an examination of how scores are used in these contexts and whether those scores differ from credit scores sold to consumers is beyond the scope of this report.

[10] A description of how scoring models are developed is available in the Appendix.

[11] The TowerGroup estimates that 9.9 billion scores were purchased, across the credit life cycle, in 2010. FICO states that it sold 9.2 billion scores for those same uses in 2010. These figures are from interviews with executive at TowerGroup and FICO. They exclude scores purchased for testing and development purposes.

[12] For example, BEACON is a FICO score used by Equifax, FICO® Risk Score, Classic by TransUnion, and Experian / Fair Isaac Risk Model by Experian. See FICO, FICO Score (online at www.fico.com/en/Products/Scoring/Pages/FICO- score.aspx) (accessed June 27, 2011).

[13] For example, credit reports used in Fannie Mae's automated underwriting system must contain specific versions of the FICO Score. See Fannie Mae, Credit Report Requirements in Desktop Underwriter (Mar. 25, 2009) (online at

www.efanniemae.com/sf/technologyFreddie Mac has similar requirements for various mortgage products. See, e.g., Freddie Mac, Requirements for Using FICO Scores for Manually Underwritten Mortgages, Freddie Mac Bulletin, at 3, No. 2010-23 (Oct. 15, 2010) (online at www.freddiemac.com/sell/guide/bulletins/pdf/bll1023.pdf).

[14] See, e.g., Department of Housing and Urban Development: Federal Housing Administration Mortgage and Loan Insurance Programs, at B-6 (2011) (online at www.hud.gov/offices/cfo/reports/2011/cjs/fha_fund_2011.pdf).

[15] See, e.g., Equifax, Things You Should Know... (online at https://help.equifax.com/app/answers/detail/a_id/386) ("The Equifax Credit Score ... is intended for your own educational use. There are numerous credit scores and models available in the marketplace and lenders may use a different score when evaluating your creditworthiness."); Experian.com (online at www.experian.com) ("Experian Credit Score indicates your relative credit risk level for educational purposes and is not the score used by lenders.").

[16] Equifax, Equifax Credit Score: What Is the Equifax Credit Score? (online at https://help.equifax.com/app/answers/detail/a_id/242/noIntercept/1/kw/equifax%20credit%20score).

[17] Experian, FAQ: What is a PLUS Score (online at www.nationalscore.com/FAQ.aspx).

[18] CreditKarma, Get Your 100% Free Credit Score! (online at www.creditkarma.com/preview/score/).

[19] For example, such variations may occur if a lender furnished account information about a consumer to one CRA but not to another.

[20] VantageScore, VantageScore 2.0 Now Available for Lender Use: Equifax, Experian, and TransUnion Implement New Scoring Model (Jan. 20, 2011) (online at www.vantagescore.com/docs/VantageScore2.0_Implementation_Release.01.20.11.pdf); VantageScore, Results from VantageScore Solutions Third Revalidation of the VantageScore Model Reflect a Trend Toward Continued Predictiveness, Consistency, Stability: Model Again Outperformed the Generic Credit Scoring Models of Three [CRAs]—Equifax, Experian and TransUnion (Oct. 16, 2007) (online at www.vantagescore.com/docs/vantagescore_press_release_101607.pdf).

[21] These are CFPB estimates, based on industry interviews and analysis of public filings, including Experian, 2011 Annual Report: Growth Through Global Strength (online at www.experianplc.com/investor-centre/reports/investor- reports/~/media/Files/E/Experian/pdf/investor/reports/2011/experian-ar-2011.pdf) and Equifax, 2010 Annual Report: Growth Through Innovation and Execution (online at www.equifax.com/shareholders

[22] 15 U.S.C. § 1681g(d); see also 16 C.F.R. Pt. 698, App. E; 15 U.S.C. § 1681m(a) (effective July 21, 2011).

[23] Letter from John W. Blenke, Executive Vice President, Corporate General Counsel and Corporate Secretary, TransUnion, LLC, to Office of the Secretary, Federal Trade Commission (Dec. 4, 2009) (online at www.ftc.gov/os/comments/freeannualfilenprm/545091-01129.pdf).

[24] See 15 U.S.C. § 1681j (f)(1); 15 U.S.C. § 1681g(f). This provision mirrors a 2001 California law requiring consumer access to a credit score for a reasonable fee. Cal. Civil Code § 1785.15.1, 1785.15.2.

[25] Similar "credit monitoring" services are also sometimes provided to consumers for free when a financial or other service provider has experienced an information security breach that may expose their customers to a risk of identity theft. In these cases the affected company may notify the consumer of the breach and voluntarily offer the service for a period of time following the notice. The services sometimes include the provision of credit reports from one or more of the CRAs, and may or may not include credit scores. See, e.g., Shan Li, SEC Data Breach Is Revealed; Payroll Information for 4,000 Agency Workers Was Sent in an Unencrypted Email, Los Angeles Times, at B2 (May 19, 2011) (regarding an offering of 60 days of free credit monitoring); see generally Data Security and Breach Notification Act of 2011, S. 1207, 112th Congress (legislation introduced to require notice to consumers of data security breaches in certain circumstances).

[26] Javelin Strategy, 2010 Annual Identity Protection Services Scorecard (2010).

[27] For example, two leading credit monitoring sites, FreeCreditScore.com and FreeCreditReport.com, are owned and operated by Experian.

[28] The CFPB believes the largest such third-party marketing companies offering credit monitoring services include Affinion, Intersections, and Vertrue.

[29] Ann Carrns, M&T Bank Offers Access to FICO Credit Score for a Fee, New York Times Bucks Blog (June 14, 2011) (online at http://bucks.blogs

[30] FICO and Experian do have agreements covering the sale of Experian credit reports with FICO scores to lenders.

[31] See generally CreditXpert.com (online at www.creditxpert.com).

[32] The Federal Reserve Board and the Federal Trade Commission have issued final rules implementing the changes to section 615(h) of the FCRA, 15 U.S.C. § 1681m(h), as amended by section 1100F of the Dodd-Frank Act. The following discussion and all citations concern these final rules. See Federal Reserve System & Federal Trade Commission, 76 Fed. Reg. 41602 (July 15, 2011) (final rules) (online at www.gpo.gov/fdsys/pkg/FR-2011-07-15/pdf/2011-17649.pdf) (this final rule will become effective thirty days after publication in the federal register); Federal Reserve System, 76 Fed. Reg. 41590 (July 15, 2011) (final rules) (online at www.gpo.gov/fdsys/pkg/FR-2011-07-15/pdf/2011-17585.pdf) (same).

[33] See, e.g., 12 C.F.R. § 222.72(a)(2) (for all lenders).

[34] See, e.g., 12 C.F.R. § 222.74(e)(ii) (for all lenders); 12 C.F.R. § 222.74(d)(ii) (for lenders who engage in risk-based pricing for a loan securing residential real property of between one and four units).

[35] 15 U.S.C. § 1681g(g)(1). These requirements were in place prior to the enactment of the Dodd-Frank Act and closely mirror a prior requirement in California law enacted effective July 1, 2001. Cal. Civ Code § 1785.15.2.

[36] 15 C.F.R. § 222.73(a)(1) and 15 C.F.R. § 222.74(d)(ii).

[37] 15 U.S.C. § 1681m(a).

[38] 15 U.S.C. § 1681g(g).

[39] Federal Reserve System & Federal Trade Commission, 75 Fed. Reg. 2724 (Jan. 15, 2010) (final rules) (online at www.ftc.gov/os/fedreg/2010/january/100115faircreditreporting.pdf).

[40] See 15 U.S.C. § 1681m(a).

[41] "I watched my score for about eight months before buying a home. I was trying to bring my credit score up and also wanted to make sure I was aware of activity on my credit report." Creditscore.com, Customer Testimonial (online at www.creditscore.com) (accessed June 27, 2011).

[42] See FICO, Take the FICO Fitness Challenge for 2011 (online at http://ficoforums.myfico.com/t5/TAKE-THE-FICO- FITNESS-CHALLENGE/Take-the-FICO-Fitness-Challenge-for-2011/td-p/812042) (showing over 600 posts by individuals during 2011 discussing how to improve their FICO score) (accessed June 27, 2011).

[43] Consumer Federation of America, New National Survey Reveals What Consumers Know and Don't Know About Changing Credit Score Marketplace (Feb. 28, 2011) (online at www.consumerfed.org/pdfs/Credit-Scores-Vantage-PR-2-28-11.pdf) (hereinafter "Consumer Federation of America Study"). The U.S. Government Accountability Office released a survey of consumers' knowledge of credit reports and credit scoring in March 2005. This survey found fairly good knowledge of basic information about credit reporting and scoring, but less knowledge of detailed questions, such as naming a number that fell in a typical scoring range. U.S. Government Accountability Office, Credit Reporting Literacy: Consumers Understood the Basics but Could Benefit from Targeted Educational Efforts (Mar. 2005) (online at www.gao.gov/new.items/d05223.pdf).

[44] The question asked consumers what the best credit score was from a series of numerical choices and gave as an option the correct answer: "Depends on the scoring system." Only 41 percent chose the correct answer. Consumer Federation of America Study, supra note 43.

[45] Id.

[46] The sample will be constructed independently, and therefore will not consist of the same 200,000 individuals at each of the three CRAs. The sample of consumer files from each CRA will include files that have at least one trade line (the term used to describe a loan or credit relationship that has been reported to the consumer reporting agency); hence, they will not be representative of the CRA's entire consumer database, which includes consumer files containing no trade lines, such as files that consist only of an inquiry or a public record item.

[47] The specific scores that will be provided are the credit score the CRA provides to consumers when selling a credit score to a consumer after the consumer has requested a consumer file disclosure through AnnualCreditReport.com, the credit score the CRA has most frequently provided in its business(es) of selling credit reports and credit scores to consumers via its branded websites or via third-party direct marketing partners, a generic FICO score, a Vantage Score, a credit card industry FICO score, and an auto-finance industry FICO score.

[48] 15 U.S.C. § 1681(f)(1)(C).

[49] The process of building a custom scoring model is similar, although the performance data will typically come from the lender's records of its own customers.

[50] For example, if at some point during the performance period a consumer were 90 days late on a payment, that information would be reflected in the data from the second snapshot.

[51] Board of Governors of the Federal Reserve System, Report to the Congress on Credit Scoring and Its Effects on the Availability and Affordability of Credit: Submitted to the Congress Pursuant to Section 215 of the Fair and Accurate Credit Transactions Act of 2003, at 18-19 n.23 (Aug. 2007) (online at www.federalreserve.gov/boarddocs/rptcongress/creditscore/creditscore.pdf).

In: Credit Scores
Editor: Phillip B. Rogers

ISBN: 978-1-62618-310-0

Chapter 2

Analysis of Differences between Consumer- and Creditor-Purchased Credit Scores*

Consumer Financial Protection Bureau

Executive Summary

When consumers purchase their credit scores from one of the major nationwide consumer reporting agencies (CRAs), they often receive scores that are not generated by the scoring models use to generate scores sold to lenders.

The Dodd-Frank Wall Street Reform and Consumer Protection Act directed the Consumer Financial Protection Bureau (CFPB) to compare credit scores sold to creditors and those sold to consumers by nationwide CRAs and determine whether differences between those scores disadvantage consumers. CFPB analyzed credit scores from 200,000 credit files from each of the three major nationwide CRAs: TransUnion, Equifax, and Experian. The study yielded the following results:

---

* This is an edited, reformatted and augmented version of the Consumer Financial Protection Bureau, dated September 2012.

- The CFPB found that for a majority of consumers the scores produced by different scoring models provided similar information about the relative creditworthiness of the consumers. That is, if a consumer had a good score from one scoring model the consumer likely had a good score on another model. For a substantial minority, however, different scoring models gave meaningfully different results.
- Correlations across the results of scoring models were high, generally over .90 (out of a possible one). Correlations were stronger among the models for consumers with scores below the median than for consumers with scores above the median.
- To determine if score variations would lead to meaningful differences between the consumers' and lenders' assessment of credit quality, the study divided scores into four credit-quality categories. The study found that different scoring models would place consumers in the same credit-quality category 73-80% of the time. Different scoring models would place consumers in credit-quality categories that are off by one category 19-24% of the time. And from 1% to 3% of consumers would be placed in categories that were two or more categories apart.
- The study looked at results within several demographic subgroups. Different scores did not appear to treat different groups of consumers systematically differently than other scoring models. The study found less variation among scores for younger consumers and consumers who live in lower-income or high-minority population ZIP codes than for older consumers or consumers in higher- income or lower-minority population ZIP codes. This is likely driven by differences in the median scores of these different categories of consumers.
- Consumers cannot know ahead of time whether the scores they purchase will closely track or vary moderately or significantly from a score sold to creditors. Thus, consumers should not rely on credit scores they purchase exclusively as a guide to how creditors will view their credit quality.
- Firms that sell scores to consumers should make consumers aware that the scores consumers purchase could vary, sometimes substantially, from the scores used by creditors.

1. INTRODUCTION

Section 1078 of the Dodd-Frank Wall Street Reform and Consumer Protection Act directs the Consumer Financial Protection Bureau (CFPB) to conduct a study on the "*nature, range, and size of variations between the credit scores sold to creditors and those sold to consumers by consumer reporting agencies that compile and maintain files on consumers on a nationwide basis ... and whether such variations disadvantage consumers.*"[1]

On July 19, 2011, the CFPB published a report on "*The impact of differences between consumer- and creditor- purchased credit scores.*" That report provided a description of the credit scoring industry; of the types of credit scores that are sold to consumers and businesses; and of the potential problems for consumers of having discrepancies between the scores they purchase and the scores used for decision-making by lenders in the marketplace.

That report also outlined a data analysis to be undertaken by the CFPB to describe credit score variations on approximately 200,000 credit files from three nationwide consumer reporting agencies (CRAs) – TransUnion, Equifax, and Experian – using credit scores typically sold to consumers and to creditors. This second report presents the findings of this analysis.

1.1. Overview of Score Variations and Why They Might Matter

As described in the July 2011 CFPB study, when a consumer purchases a score from a nationwide CRA, it is likely that the credit score will not be the same as the score used by a particular lender or other commercial credit report user in making a lending or other score-based decision with respect to that consumer. The variation in scores reflects not only differences between scores sold to consumer and scores sold to creditors, but also differences among scores sold to creditors.

1.1.1. Types of Scores

Lenders use a wide variety of credit scores which vary by score provider, by model, and by target industry.

1.1.1.a. FICO Scores

One consulting firm estimates that scores developed by Fair Isaac Corporation (FICO) accounted for over 90% of the market of scores sold to firms in 2010 for use in credit-related decisions.[2] There are numerous FICO scoring models that vary by version (e.g., newer and older models), by the nationwide CRA that sells the score to lenders, and by industry.

FICO's most current model is FICO 08, but commercial users still use earlier versions of FICO products. Additionally, FICO's generic scoring models – the most common FICO scores that are developed to predict performance on all types of credit - vary across the nationwide CRAs because the FICO scoring models are designed specifically for each CRA and reflect differences in how they organize and present credit report data.

FICO offers industry-specific models for credit cards, mortgages, auto loans, and telecommunication services. FICO models typically generate credit scores in the range between 300 and 850. FICO also builds custom models that are designed for specific companies' credit underwriting needs.

1.1.1.b. Vantage Scores

VantageScore LLC, a score development company established as a joint venture of Equifax, TransUnion, and Experian, licenses its scoring models for sale by the three nationwide CRAs to both creditors and consumers. There are currently two Vantage scoring models in use: VantageScore and VantageScore 2.0. The original VantageScore® launched in 2006. VantageScore 2.0, developed using data from 2006 to 2009, launched in October 2010. The VantageScore models produce scores in the range of 501-990.

1.1.1.c. Consumer Reporting Agency Scores

CRAs are companies that gather, organize, standardize, and disseminate consumer information, especially credit information. Each of the nationwide CRAs – Equifax, TransUnion, and Experian - have their own proprietary generic scoring models to predict credit performance. These models were originally developed for use by lenders to predict performance on credit obligations, but are now primarily sold as educational scores to consumers.[3] These scores typically resemble FICO scores in range. Some of the proprietary generic scores sold by the CRAs are:

- Equifax: "Equifax Credit Score." Produces scores in the range 280-850.[4]
- Experian: "Experian Plus Score." Produces scores in the range 330-830.[5]
- TransUnion: "TransRisk New Account Score." Produces scores in the range 300-850.[6]

In addition to being sold to consumers on a stand-alone basis, educational scores are often the scores provided by the CRAs to consumers who have purchased or otherwise subscribed to credit monitoring services, which typically provide reports and scores on a regular basis.

1.1.2. Consumer Purchases of Credit Scores

While consumers can obtain free annual credit reports from the nationwide CRAs, they typically have to pay for credit scores.[7] Consumers purchase scores through several channels. In most cases, the scores consumers purchase are educational credit scores made available to them by the nationwide CRAs and through other channels. Consumers may purchase scores by contacting a nationwide CRA directly or by purchasing a score to accompany the free credit reports consumers are able to obtain annually at annualcreditreport.com. The nationwide CRAs generally sell consumers educational scores or VantageScore scores. Consumers can also obtain credit scores by subscribing to credit monitoring services. Again, these scores are typically educational. Some educational credit scoring providers make scores available to consumers for free.

In some circumstances consumers can purchase FICO scores. For example, Equifax offers a FICO score for sale with an Equifax credit report, and consumers' FICO scores derived from credit reports from both Equifax and TransUnion can be purchased from FICO's consumer website, myfico.com. Consumers cannot purchase a FICO score generated from an Experian credit report. Even where a consumer purchases a FICO score and goes to a creditor that uses FICO scores, the score may not be the one any particular creditor uses, given the diversity of scores in the marketplace and the possibility that the creditor may obtain scores from a different CRA.

1.1.3. Potential Harms for Consumers

Variations between the credit scores sold to consumers and to lenders carry significance only if such variations lead to consumer harms. The July 19, 2011 CFPB Report highlighted potential harms for consumers. These harms include those resulting from consumers' inaccurate perceptions of their own credit worthiness.

1.1.3.a. Harms from Inaccurate Perception of Creditworthiness

A consumer can face harms if, after purchasing a credit score, the consumer has a different impression of his or her creditworthiness than a lender would. If the score leads the consumer to overestimate lenders' likely assessment of his or her creditworthiness, the consumer might be likely to apply for credit lines that would not be approved, with a cost of wasted time and effort on both the consumer's and lender's part. Alternatively, the consumer may reject offers of credit that would be beneficial because the consumer's misperception of his or her creditworthiness leads the consumer to believe that the offers are over-priced.

If a consumer underestimates lenders' likely assessment of his or her creditworthiness, the consumer might fail to apply for credit at all or delay applying for credit, forgoing the opportunity to buy a house or car, for example, or delaying a valuable mortgage refinancing. A consumer might also apply to lenders who offer less favorable terms than he or she might qualify for, or accept less favorable offers received through the mail or online direct marketing. In this case, the cost to the affected consumer would be higher interest costs and possibly higher likelihoods of default due to the greater costs and difficulty of making monthly payments. Lenders might benefit by being able to charge higher interest to consumers who "incorrectly" understand their options when applying; at the same time lenders would lose out on business from consumers who decide not to apply for credit due to a misperception of its likely cost. Finally, consumers who believe their credit score to be low may take costly steps that they believe may improve their credit score.

1.1.3.b. Small differences, Big impacts

Notably, the potential for a consumer to be confused may be greater where the consumer is sophisticated about the use of credit scores by creditors. Many lenders use specific score levels as thresholds to determine whether consumers will qualify for a particular loan or interest rate. For example, FICO score levels 620, 680, and 740 might be used by a lender as the boundary lines between consumers considered to be "sub-prime, "near-prime," or "prime" credit risks, respectively. A striking example of this is the fact that Fannie Mae generally won't buy mortgages with FICO scores under 620.[8] So, for consumers whose scores are in the relevant range, a small variation in a consumer's score might result in his or her score falling above or below such a cut-off, with dramatic implications for his or her access to home loans. Given the use of score thresholds to determine eligibility for certain products or pricing tiers, even small variations can have large impacts for certain consumers. If a consumer believes incorrectly that he falls above or below a crucial threshold then the impact of a given difference between scores may be magnified, since it may be more likely to have an impact on the consumer's perceptions and consequent credit-seeking behavior.

1.1.4. Study Objectives

To explore these issues, the CFPB undertook this follow-up study to the July 19, 2011 CFPB Report on credit scores to examine scores sold to consumers and see how well they correlate with the scores used by lenders.

2. Analysis and Results

This chapter of the report describes the data analyzed and presents results of several approaches to analyzing differences and similarities across scoring models.

The CFPB found that for a majority of consumers the scores produced by different scoring models provide similar information about the relative creditworthiness of the consumers. That is, if a consumer had a good score from one scoring model the consumer likely had a good score on another model. For a substantial minority, however, different scoring models gave meaningfully different results.

2.1. Data

Each of the three larger nationwide CRAs, Equifax, Experian, and TransUnion, provided the CFPB with a random sample of 200,000 consumer reports and credit scores calculated on such reports. The samples were chosen independently at the three CRAs; the samples were not designed to contain the same individuals. The samples selected included only reports with at least one trade line – and not, for example, simply an inquiry – that therefore would be potentially "scoreable" by at least one scoring model.

For each consumer report in the sample, the CRAs provided five credit scores; the file's trade line history, scrubbed of any potentially personally identifiable information; and ZIP code and age information to allow the CFPB to compare scores by consumer demographics.[9]

The five credit scores provided by each nationwide CRA for the study were:

1. The generic FICO[10] score sold by the CRA. Equifax provided BEACON 5, a FICO score; Experian provided FICO V2 (Quest); and TransUnion provided FICO Classic 2004.

2. The CRA's educational score sold to consumers. Equifax provided EquifaxRisk 3.0 scores, Experian provided Experian PLUS scores, and TransUnion provided TransRisk New Account Scores.
3. VantageScore 1.0.
4. FICO Auto Loan industry-specific score.
5. FICO BankCard industry-specific score.

The FICO scores and VantageScore are all sold to creditors. The generic FICO score (in some circumstances), the VantageScore, and the educational scores are sold to consumers. There are therefore a number of potential situations where the consumer could purchase a score and a creditor could purchase a different score to evaluate the creditworthiness of that consumer. The situations that can be evaluated with the data are: the consumer buys an educational score and the creditor uses a FICO score; the consumer buys an educational score and the creditor uses a VantageScore; the consumer buys a VantageScore and the creditor uses a FICO score; and, the consumer buys a FICO score and the creditor uses a VantageScore. Note that the last two situations are symmetric, and therefore there are three relevant pair-wise comparisons for each of the analyses: educational versus FICO, educational versus VantageScore, and VantageScore versus FICO. Analysis showed that the industry-specific scores are very highly correlated to the generic FICO scores, and therefore comparisons with those models are not presented – results were very similar to analysis of the generic FICO score.[11]

The results of the analysis were extremely similar qualitatively across the three CRAs. The study therefore presents results from a single CRA in the body of the report and provides results for the other two CRAs in the Appendix. There is one exception to this broader pattern. The sample provided by one of the CRAs contained very few young consumers because of the way the sample was drawn. Adjusting for this difference (e.g., focusing on older consumers) the results for this CRA are very similar to the other two CRAs.[12]

2.2. Analysis and Results

2.2.1. Score Distributions

In order to better understand differences in scores across models, and in anticipation of some of the results shown later in the report, it is useful to have some background on the distribution of scores across consumers.

In addition to the score range that score developers select, developers determine the shape of the distribution of scores. This is because scores rank consumers according to their relative risk and therefore the relationship between score and absolute risk does not have to be constant across the score range. Figure 1 shows the score distributions for the three models for one of the CRAs. It shows that the FICO score and the educational score are scaled such that there is a large proportion of scores in the higher end and a long "tail" at the lower end of the score distribution, while the VantageScore is scaled such that the distribution of scores is relatively flat across the score distribution. This means that small changes in a FICO score or educational score at the high end of the score distribution translate into relatively large percentile changes, while changes in score at the low end of the FICO or educational score range translate into relatively small percentile changes. For VantageScore, on the other hand, a given score change leads to a similar percentage change across the score distribution.

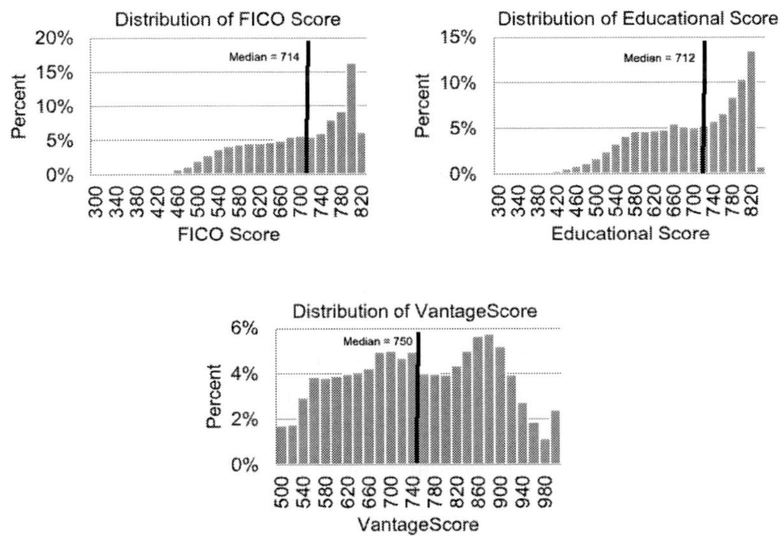

Figure 1. Score Distributions.

All credit scoring models rank individual consumers by their *relative* credit risk. That is, a score represents a consumer's likelihood of becoming delinquent on a loan *relative to the risk of other consumers who represent lower risks (i.e., have higher scores) or higher risk (i.e., have lower scores).* For a given population and time period, however, absolute default probabilities can be calculated. Figure 2 shows an example of default risk by FICO score. It shows that at the low end of the score range the risk of default is very high and the relationship between score and risk is fairly steep, while at the high of the score distribution, where risk is very low, the relationship is fairly flat. This means that score differences at the low end of the score distribution are associated with relatively large differences in default probability, while score differences at the high end are associated with relatively small differences in default probability.

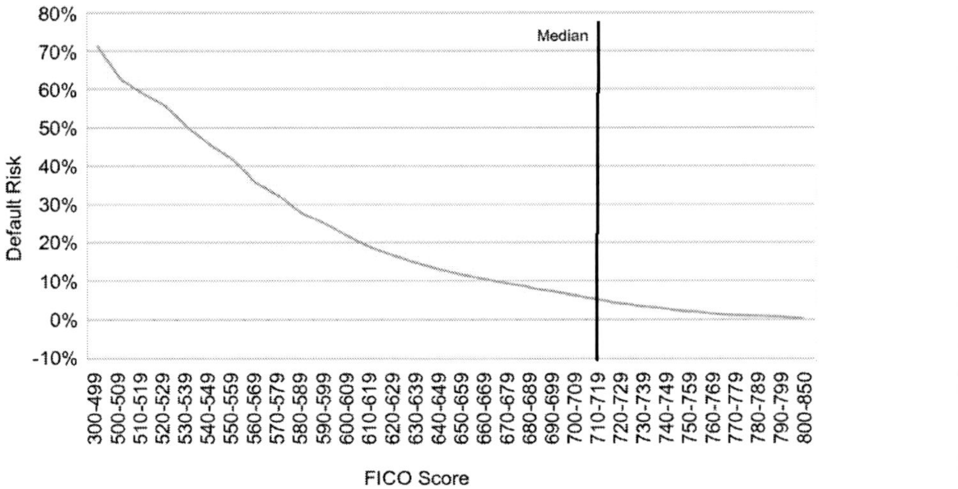

Figure 2. Default Risk by Fico Score[13].

2.2.2. Adjusting for Score Range Differences

As discussed in the introduction, different scoring models use different ranges. FICO scores have a 300-850 range, educational scores resemble the FICO range with minor variations, and VantageScore ranges from 500-990. In order to make useful comparisons across scoring models the scores were first converted into a relative score. This was done separately for each scoring model. Consumers were first ranked by score. Their percentile in the distribution of scores was then determined, and this was the "relative score" used throughout the analysis. For example, consider a consumer with a FICO score of 680. The score places the consumer at the 38th percentile of the FICO score distribution, meaning he or she has a better FICO score than 38% of consumers. His or her relative score for the FICO model was therefore 38. This was also done for the VantageScore and the educational score. This allowed us to compare where consumers fell in the score distribution using each of the models, and disentangle these differences from the differences that arose because different scoring models use different score ranges. We use the phrase "relative score" to mean the percentile equivalent of the score generated by a particular model.

2.2.3. Correlation across Scoring Models

The simplest measure of similarity or difference of the scores produced by the different scoring models is "correlation." Correlation is a measure of how closely related two variables are, and ranges from -1 to 1. A value of -1 indicates that two variables have a perfectly inverse relationship, while a value of 1 means they are perfectly related. A value of zero means that there is no relationship between the two variables. So, the closer the correlation between the scores produced by two models is to 1, the tighter the relationship between those scoring models, and the more similar the two scores will be for a given consumer (on average).

Figure 3 provides visual representations of these relationships. It shows "scatter-plot" graphs that show consumers' relative scores from pairs of scoring models. A dot represents consumers with the given combination of scores (as shown on the axes); dot size shows the relative number of consumers that have a given combinations of scores. (The "lumpiness" in the figures arises from using percentiles; there were some score "ties" that lead to more than 1% of consumers being assigned the same score percentile.) These figures each showed clearly that there is a relationship between the scores produced by these models for each consumer, but scores were not perfectly correlated. Figure 3 also shows that there appeared to be greater dispersion between the pairs of scores above the median, so that scores were more similar for consumers with worse scores and less similar for consumers with better scores.

Figure 4 shows the correlations for each of the pairs of scoring models. It shows that the correlations were high, in each case equal to or greater than 0.9. Figure 4 also shows the correlations when the sample was split into low-score and high-score groups, using the average percentile across the two groups and splitting at the median (the 50th percentile). It confirms what is apparent from the figure, that scores, as measured by score percentile, were less closely correlated for high-score consumers than low-score consumers.

Figure 2 provides some insight into why scores were more highly correlated for low-score consumers than for high-score consumers. As shown in Figure 2, there was much less variation in default risk above the median (ranging from roughly 0% to 5%) than below (where it ranges from roughly 5% to over 60%). This is true for VantageScore as well, as shown in Appendix Figure 2. Consequently, it is not surprising that different scoring models tended to "agree" more on the scores for consumers below the median. It is easier to statistically distinguish a consumer that poses, e.g., a 20% default risk from a consumer that poses a 10% default risk than it is to distinguish a consumer that poses a 2% default risk from a consumer that poses a 1% default risk.

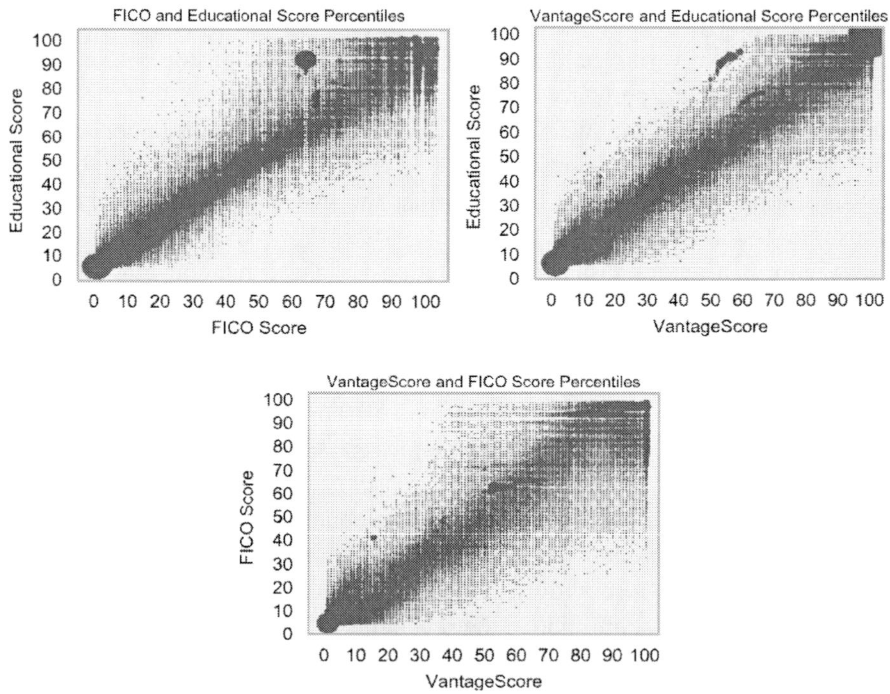

Figure 3. Scatterplots.

	Overall	Customers Below Median		Customers Above Median
FICO vs. Educational	0.93	0.86	>	0.64
Vantage vs. Educational	0.93	0.82	>	0.68
Vantage vs. FICO	0.90	0.77	>	0.52

Figure 4. Score Correlations.

Educational vs. FICO	Rank for FICO Score										
Rank for Educational Score	<10%	<20%	<30%	<40%	<50%	<60%	<70%	<80%	<90%	<100%	All
<100%			0%	0%	0%	0%	1%	2%	3%	4%	10%
<90%		0%	0%	0%	0%	0%	1%	2%	3%	3%	11%
<80%		0%	0%	0%	0%	1%	2%	3%	3%	2%	10%
<70%		0%	0%	0%	1%	2%	3%	3%	1%	0%	10%
<60%	0%	0%	0%	1%	2%	4%	2%	1%	0%	0%	10%
<50%	0%	0%	1%	3%	4%	2%	0%	0%	0%	0%	10%
<40%	0%	1%	2%	5%	2%	0%	0%	0%	0%		10%
<30%	1%	3%	4%	2%	0%	0%	0%				9%
<20%	2%	5%	2%	0%	0%	0%					10%
<10%	7%	2%	0%	0%							10%
All	10%	10%	10%	10%	10%	9%	9%	10%	11%	10%	100%

VantageScore vs. Educational	Rank for Educational Score										
Rank for VantageScore	<10%	<20%	<30%	<40%	<50%	<60%	<70%	<80%	<90%	<100%	All
<100%			0%	0%	0%	0%	0%	1%	3%	5%	10%
<90%			0%	0%	0%	0%	1%	2%	4%	3%	10%
<80%		0%	0%	0%	0%	1%	2%	3%	3%	1%	10%
<70%			0%	0%	1%	2%	4%	2%	1%	0%	10%
<60%		0%	0%	1%	2%	3%	2%	1%	1%	0%	10%
<50%	0%	0%	1%	2%	4%	2%	1%	0%	0%	0%	10%
<40%	0%	1%	2%	4%	3%	1%	0%	0%	0%		10%
<30%	1%	2%	4%	2%	0%	0%	0%	0%			10%
<20%	3%	4%	2%	1%	0%	0%	0%				10%
<10%	6%	3%	1%	0%	0%						10%
All	10%	10%	10%	10%	10%	10%	10%	10%	10%	10%	100%

VantageScore vs. FICO	Rank for FICO Score										
Rank for VantageScore	<10%	<20%	<30%	<40%	<50%	<60%	<70%	<80%	<90%	<100%	All
<100%		0%	0%	0%	0%	0%	1%	2%	3%	3%	10%
<90%			0%	0%	0%	1%	1%	2%	3%	4%	10%
<80%		0%		0%	1%	1%	1%	3%	3%	2%	10%
<70%	0%	0%	0%	0%	1%	2%	3%	2%	1%	1%	10%
<60%	0%	0%	0%	1%	2%	3%	3%	1%	0%	0%	10%
<50%	0%	0%	1%	3%	3%	2%	1%	0%	0%	0%	10%
<40%	0%	1%	2%	4%	2%	1%	0%	0%	0%	0%	10%
<30%	1%	3%	3%	2%	0%	0%	0%	0%		0%	10%
<20%	3%	3%	2%	0%	0%	0%	0%	0%			9%
<10%	6%	3%	1%	0%	0%						10%
All	10%	10%	10%	10%	10%	9%	9%	10%	11%	10%	100%

Figure 5. Decile Comparisons.

2.2.4. Magnitude of Differences across Scoring Models

The correlation and the scatter-plots show that scores were generally similar across scoring models. What they do not make clear is how many consumers had very similar scores across the different models and how many had large differences in their scores. To evaluate this, consumers were divided up into score categories, and then the categories that consumers fall into using the different scoring models were compared. The categories used are "deciles," groups of 10% of the sample.[14] For example, consumers with

VantageScores in the bottom 10% of scores, consumers with scores between the 10th percentile of scores and the 20th percentile of scores, etc.

Figure 5 shows the results of comparing score deciles across scoring models. Note that cells with entries of "0%" have some consumers in them but so few that they round to zero, while blank cells have no consumers.

Figure 6 summarizes the results presented in Figure 5. It shows that most consumers, 78 - 86% depending on the comparison, had scores that were in the same decile or in adjacent deciles for each of the two scoring models. A sizeable minority, however, 11 - 16%, had scores that were two deciles away from each other across the scoring models, and a small number, 3 - 6%, have scores that were three or more deciles away from each other.

Educational vs. FICO		Cumulative
Decile match (green)	42% (75,592)	42% (75,592)
Adjacent deciles (light green)	43% (76,813)	85% (152,405)
Two deciles off (yellow)	11% (20,436)	97% (172,841)
Three or more deciles off (red)	3% (5,736)	100% (178,577)
Total	100% (178,577)	100% (178,577)

FICO vs. Vantage		Cumulative
Decile match (green)	34% (60,596)	34% (60,596)
Adjacent deciles (light green)	44% (78,388)	78% (138,984)
Two deciles off (yellow)	16% (28,007)	94% (166,991)
Three or more deciles off (red)	6% (10,718)	100% (177,709)
Total	100% (177,709)	100% (177,709)

Educational vs. Vantage		Cumulative
Decile match (green)	42% (76,435)	42% (76,435)
Adjacent deciles (light green)	44% (81,275)	86% (157,710)
Two deciles off (yellow)	11% (20,472)	97% (178,182)
Three or more deciles off (red)	3% (5,669)	100% (183,851)
Total	100% (183,851)	100% (183,851)

Figure 6. Decile Analysis.

2.2.5. Economically Meaningful Differences across Scoring Models

The decile comparisons show how many consumers had scores from different models that were in substantially different portions of the score distribution. These differences, however, did not necessarily translate into meaningful differences between outcomes consumers might expect, based on the scores they obtain, and actual outcomes, based on the scores that creditors actually use to evaluate them. In order to evaluate this it was necessary to identify differences between scores that would be meaningful in the marketplace. Creditors often use scores by establishing score ranges and treating consumers within a range the same for purposes of underwriting or pricing. The use of scores and score categories varies across product markets, and within product markets different creditors use scores differently. In order to evaluate how often meaningful differences would occur we divided score distributions into a set of ranges. These ranges reflect an approximation of how scores are used; this does not reflect the use of scores in any one market or by any one creditor. Consumers were categorized into different score bins for FICO scores and educational scores:

- Below 620;
- Between 620 and 680;
- Between 680 and 740; and
- Above 740.

For VantageScores, consumers were categorized by taking the percentiles associated with each of the FICO score thresholds and applying that percentile cut-point to the distributions of VantageScores. For example, a 620 FICO score is the 25th percentile of the FICO score distribution, so the lowest score category of VantageScores was made up of scores below the 25th percentile of the VantageScore distribution. Similarly, a FICO score of 680 represents the 38th percentile of scores, so the next lowest range of VantageScores was the 25th to 38th percentiles.

Figure 7 shows these comparisons for each of the pairs of scores rounded to the nearest whole percent:

Figure 8 summarizes the results from the above figures. It shows that most consumers, 73 – 80%, were in the same score categories across the different scoring models. This means that the scores consumers receive will usually give them an accurate understanding of how creditors, using another scoring model, would perceive them. Most of the remaining consumers, 19 – 24%, would likely have a moderate but meaningfully different impression of their credit score than would a creditor using the other score. A very small portion, 1 – 3%, would receive a very different impression than would a creditor using the other score. These findings rely on consumers being sophisticated enough to know how a score they receive might translate into broad pricing or underwriting categories used in the marketplace and in the particular score ranges used here. If some creditors use narrower score ranges, then a smaller share of consumers going to those creditors would have an accurate view.

2.2.6. Results for Population Subgroups

The data provided by the CRAs allows some limited analysis of sub-populations of consumers. In particular, the CRAs provided information on age and ZIP code.

While ZIP codes are relatively large areas there is still a fair amount of variation across ZIP codes in income and racial and ethnic makeup. ZIP codes were matched to 2000 Census data on income and race and ethnicity.

Educational vs. FICO	FICO Score				
Educational Score	< 620	620 - 680	680 - 740	> 740	All
>740	0%	0%	4%	39%	44%
680 – 740	0%	3%	9%	3%	15%
620 – 680	3%	9%	3%	0%	15%
< 620	23%	3%	0%	0%	26%
All	27%	15%	16%	42%	100%

Educational vs. VantageScore	Educational Score				
Rank for VantageScore	< 620	620 - 680	680 - 740	> 740	All
Over 55%	0%	0%	5%	40%	45%
< 55%	1%	5%	8%	3%	17%
< 38%	4%	7%	2%	0%	13%
< 25%	22%	3%	0%	0%	25%
All	27%	15%	16%	43%	100%

FICO vs. VantageScore	FICO Score				
Rank for VantageScore	< 620	620 - 680	680 - 740	> 740	All
Over 55%	0%	1%	7%	39%	47%
< 55%	1%	5%	7%	4%	17%
< 38%	4%	6%	2%	0%	13%
< 25%	21%	2%	0%	0%	24%
All	27%	15%	16%	43%	100%

Figure 7. Score Range Comparisons.

Figures 9 and 10 show comparisons of median score percentiles and correlations between different scoring models for consumers in different age categories, in ZIP codes with different median income, and ZIP codes with different racial and ethnic make-ups.[15] They show that different groups had very similar median scores across scoring models. For example, younger consumers[16] had lower median scores than older consumers[17], and this finding was consistent across scoring models. The median score for young consumers was very similar across models, between the 31st and 35th percentiles of the overall score distribution. Similarly, consumers who live in lower-income ZIP codes[18] and consumers who live in ZIP codes with high minority populations[19] had relatively low scores, with median scores in the mid-30s of the overall score distribution across scoring models.

FICO vs. Educational		Cumulative
Same score category (green)	80% (142,493)	80% (142,493)
Score category off by 1 (yellow)	19% (34,631)	99% (177,124)
Score category off by 2 or more (red)	1% (1,454)	100% (178,578)
Total	100% (178,578)	100% (178,578)

Educational vs. Vantage		Cumulative
Same score category (green)	77% (141,916)	77% (141,916)
Score category off by 1 (yellow)	22% (39,763)	99% (181,679)
Score category off by 2 or more (red)	1% (2,172)	100% (183,851)
Total	100% (183,851)	100% (183,851)

FICO vs. Vantage		Cumulative
Same score category (green)	73% (129,858)	73% (129,858)
Score category off by 1 (yellow)	24% (42,941)	97% (172,799)
Score category off by 2 or more (red)	3% (4,910)	100% (177,709)
Total	100% (177,709)	100% (177,709)

Figure 8. Score Range Analysis.

These findings with respect to differences in median scores by age, race and ethnicity, and income are consistent with previous analysis by other researchers, including in a detailed study by the Federal Reserve Board in a 2007 report to Congress.[20]

We do not address here the underlying causes of these differences nor the implications for different groups of consumer.

Turning to correlations, Figure 10 shows that scores were slightly more correlated for younger consumers and consumers who live in lower-income or high-minority population ZIP codes.

This result is consistent with the finding described above that scores were more highly correlated for consumers with lower scores than for consumers with higher scores.

	Educational Median	FICO Median	Vantage Median	Difference	Educational Median	FICO Median	Vantage Median	Difference
	Younger				Older			
Educational vs. FICO	35	35	-	0	74	74	-	0
Educational vs. Vantage	35	-	31	4	74	-	72	2
FICO vs. Vantage	-	35	32	-3	-	74	73	-1
	Customers in LMI Areas				Customers in Non-LMI Areas			
Educational vs. FICO	36	34	-	2	54	52	-	2
Educational vs. Vantage	35	-	35	0	53	-	53	0
FICO vs. Vantage	-	34	36	2	-	52	54	2
	Majority Minority Areas				Low Minority Areas			
Educational vs. FICO	36	34	-	2	54	52	-	2
Educational vs. Vantage	35	-	35	0	53	-	53	0
FICO vs. Vantage	-	34	37	3	-	53	55	2

Figure 9. Median Score Comparisons.

	Younger		Older
Educational vs. FICO	0.92	>	0.90
Educational vs. Vantage	0.91	>	0.90
FICO vs. Vantage	0.89	>	0.85
	Customers in LMI Areas		**Customers in Non-LMI Areas**
Educational vs. FICO	0.94	>	0.93
Educational vs. Vantage	0.93	~	0.93
FICO vs. Vantage	0.91	>	0.90
	Majority Minority Areas		**Low Minority Areas**
Educational vs. FICO	0.94	>	0.93
Educational vs. Vantage	0.93	~	0.93
FICO vs. Vantage	0.90	~	0.90

Figure 10. Median Score Correlations.

3. IMPACT AND POLICY IMPLICATIONS

This study has found that for a majority of consumers the scores produced by different scoring models provide similar information about the relative creditworthiness of the consumers. That is, if a consumer had a good score from one scoring model the consumer likely had a good score on another model. For a substantial minority, however, different scoring models gave meaningfully different results.

The study found that for 73-80% of consumers different scoring models place consumers in the same category of credit quality. Different scoring models place consumers in credit-quality categories that are off by one category 19-24% of the time. And from 1% to 3% of consumers are placed in categories that are two or more categories apart.

These findings suggest that consumers should avoid relying on scores they purchase as the sole basis for assessing their creditworthiness when making important decisions about obtaining credit. No consumer will know in advance whether the score he or she sees will vary significantly from the score a creditor sees. Thus, each consumer should be prepared for the possibility that the score he or she sees is meaningfully different from the score used by a lender.

In evaluating educational credit scores, consumers should also consider the following:

(1) **Many scores exist in the marketplace**: It is unclear the extent to which consumers understand that multiple scores exist in the marketplace. It is likely that many consumers incorrectly believe that the scores they purchase are the same scores used by lenders in evaluating their applications for credit. As described throughout this paper, literally dozens of different credit models are used by lenders. FICO alone has over 49 credit scoring models.[21] Consumers additionally can purchase a range of educational scores or VantageScores.

(2) **Consumers should check their credit reports for accuracy and dispute any errors**: Credit scores are calculated based on information in a consumer's credit file. Regardless of the credit scoring model used, inaccurate adverse information in a consumer's file (e.g. unpaid accounts that are not the consumer's, accounts described as paid late that were paid on time), can hurt that consumer's credit score. Before shopping for major credit items, consumers should review their credit

files for inaccuracies. Each of the nationwide CRAs is required by law to provide credit reports for free to consumers once every 12 months upon request. A consumer can obtain these reports at annualcreditreport.com. Consumers can get information on this and the dispute process at ask cfpb.

(3) **Consumers should shop for credit:** Regardless of variations in educational and commercial scores, or even among scoring models used by lenders (which was analyzed in this study in only a very limited and somewhat indirect manner) consumers benefit by shopping for credit. Even if provided the same score, lenders may offer different loan terms because they operate different risk models or face different competitive pressures. Consumers should not rule themselves out of seeking lower priced credit due to assumptions about their credit score.

Some consumers are reluctant to shop for credit out of fear that they will harm their credit score. Many consumers are generally aware that inquiries by creditors can negatively impact their credit score. However, the potentially negative impact of inquiries on credit scores may be overblown. For example, FICO reports that its scoring models treat multiple inquiries made for either a mortgage, auto, or student loan within the same 30 day-window as a single inquiry. Even when credit inquiries are counted separately, as in the case of credit card applications, each additional credit inquiry will take fewer than 5 points off a FICO score.[22] Other scoring models such as Vantage also do not heavily weight inquiries. An inquiry will take 1 to 5 points off a Vantage score.[23]

(4) **Providers of educational scores should ensure that the potential for score differences is clear to consumers:** This study finds that for a substantial minority of consumers, the scores that consumers purchase from the nationwide CRAs depict consumers' creditworthiness differently from the scores sold to creditors. It is likely that, unaided, many consumers will not understand this fact or even understand that the score they have obtained is an educational score and not the score that a lender is likely to rely upon. Consumers obtaining educational scores may be confused about the usefulness of the score being sold if sellers of scores do not make it clear to consumers before the consumer purchases the educational score that it is not the score the lender is likely to use.

APPENDIX

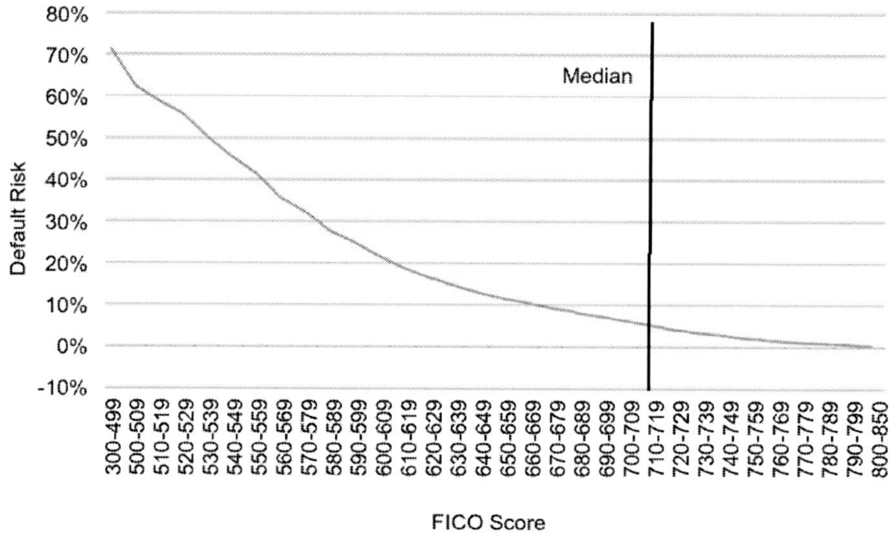

Appendix Figure 1. Default Risk by Fico Score.

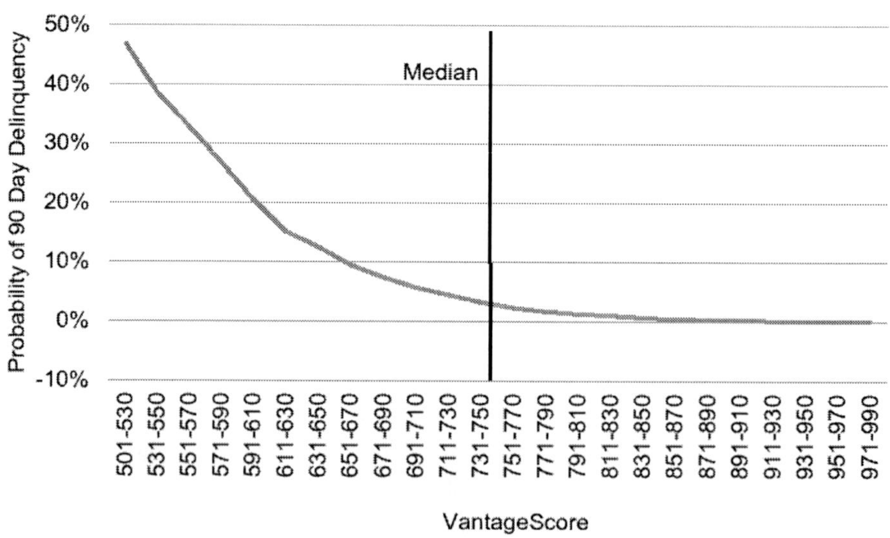

Appendix Figure 2. 90 Day Delinquency Rate by Vantagescore.

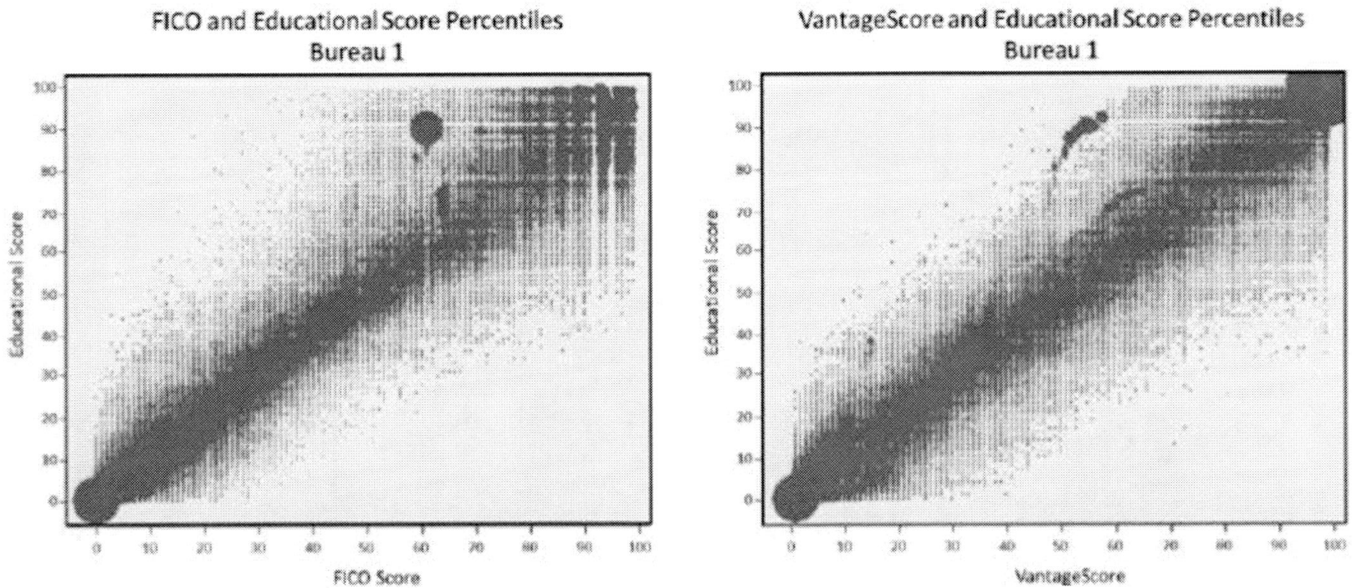

Appendix Figure 3. (Continued)

VantageScore and FICO Score Percentiles
Bureau 1

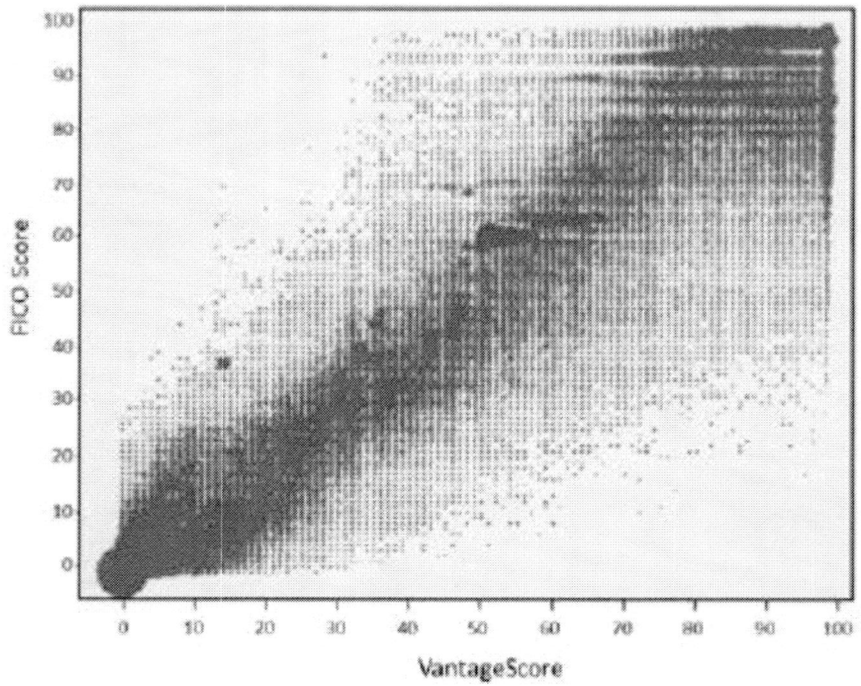

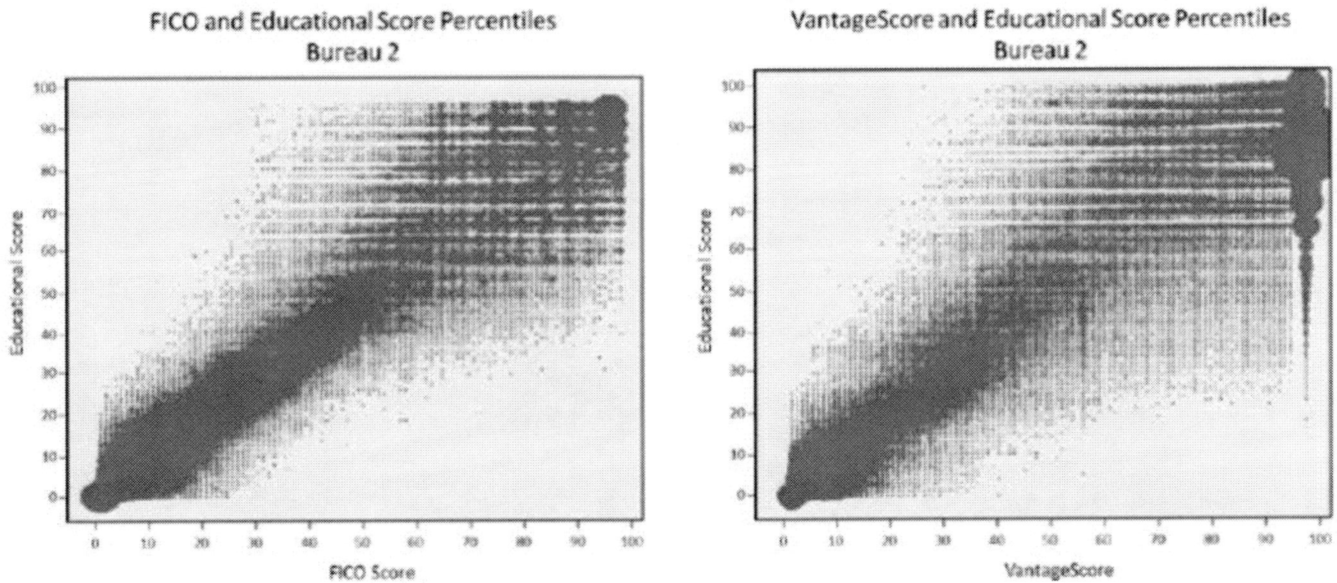

Appendix Figure 3. (Continued).

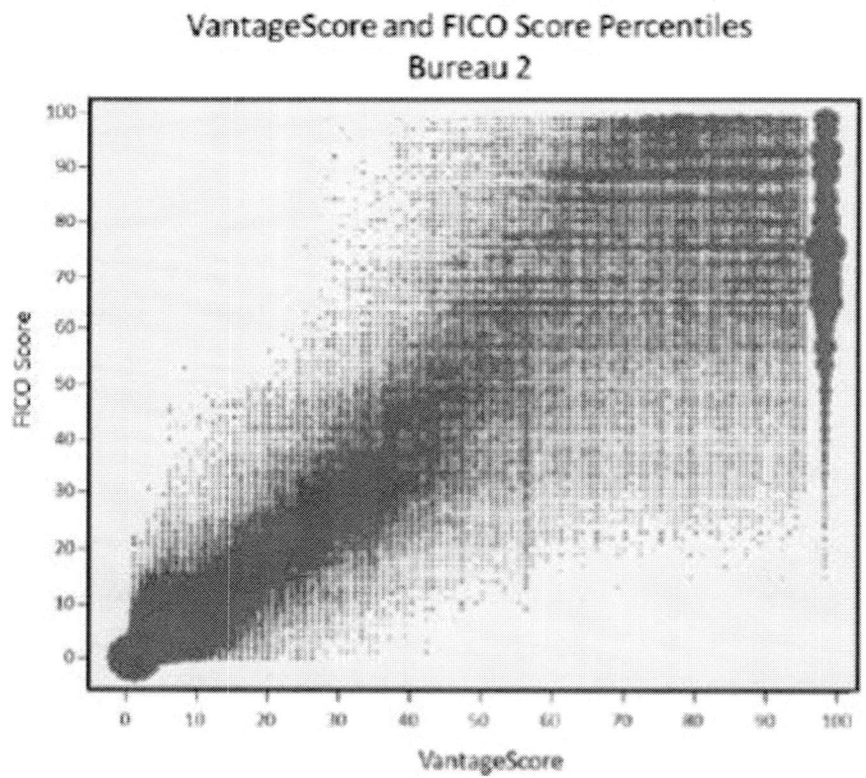
VantageScore and FICO Score Percentiles
Bureau 2
FICO Score
VantageScore
0
10
20
30
40
50
60
70
80
90
100

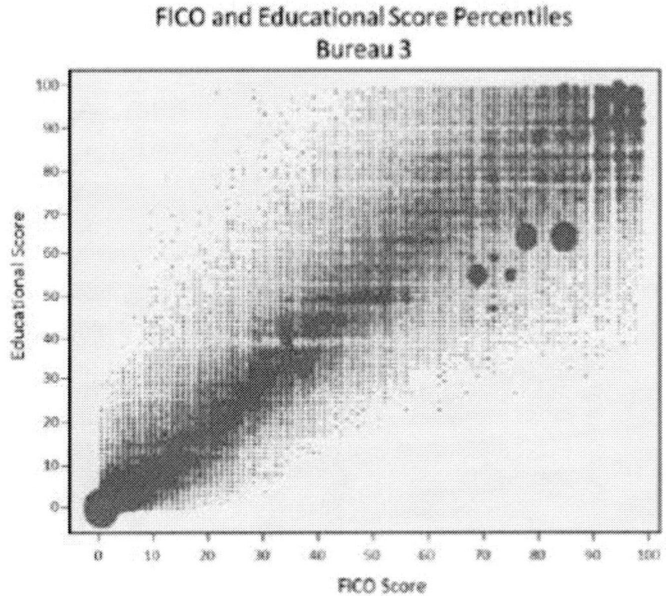

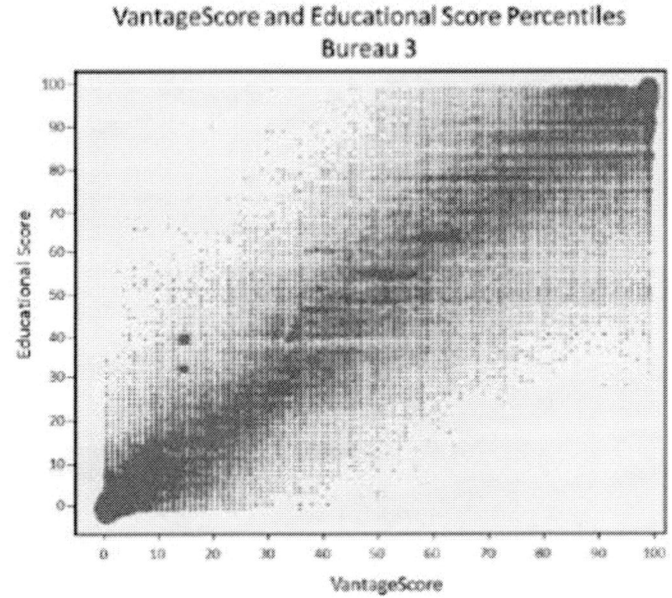

Appendix Figure 3. (Continued)

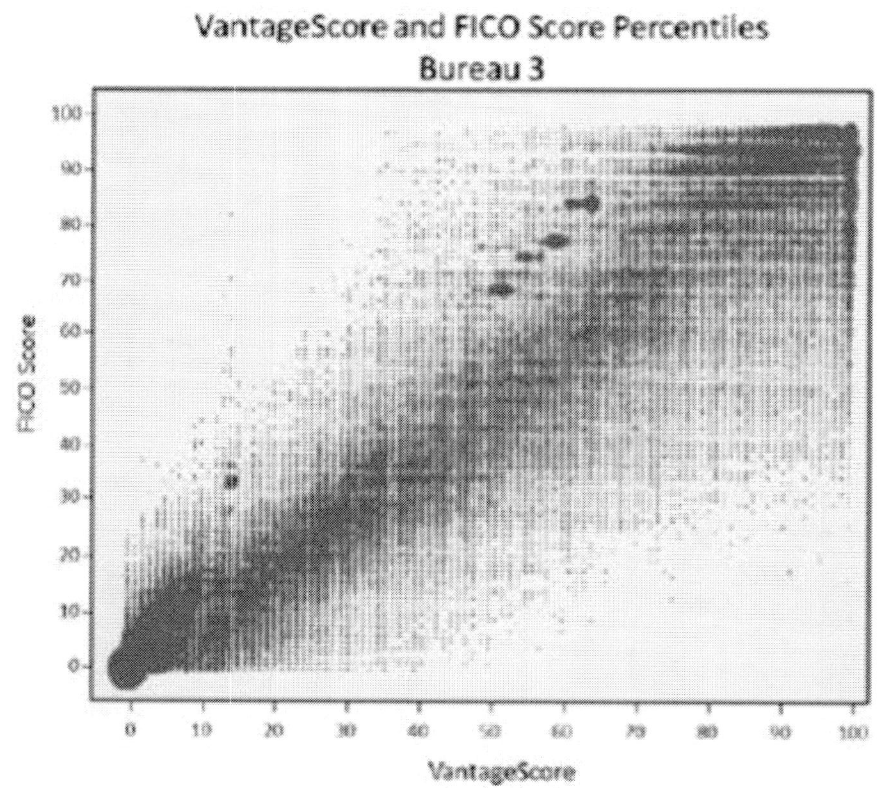

Appendix Figure 3. Scatterplots.

Bureau 1	Overall	Customers Below Median		Customers Above Median
FICO vs. Educational	0.93	0.86	>	0.64
Vantage vs. Educational	0.93	0.82	>	0.68
Vantage vs. FICO	0.90	0.77	>	0.52

Bureau 2	Overall	Customers Below Median		Customers Above Median
FICO vs. Educational	0.90	0.85	>	0.48
Vantage vs. Educational	0.85	0.77	>	0.23
Vantage vs. FICO	0.83	0.78	>	0.13

Bureau 3	Overall	Customers Below Median		Customers Above Median
FICO vs. Educational	0.92	0.84	>	0.55
Vantage vs. Educational	0.91	0.75	>	0.57
Vantage vs. FICO	0.90	0.77	>	0.49

Appendix Figure 4. Score Correlations.

Educational vs. FICO Bureau 1	Rank for FICO Score										
Rank for Educational Score	<10%	<20%	<30%	<40%	<50%	<60%	<70%	<80%	<90%	<100%	All
<100%			0%	0%	0%	0%	1%	2%	3%	4%	10%
<90%		0%	0%	0%	0%	0%	1%	2%	3%	3%	11%
<80%		0%	0%	0%	0%	1%	2%	3%	3%	2%	10%
<70%		0%	0%	0%	1%	2%	3%	3%	1%	0%	10%
<60%	0%	0%	0%	1%	2%	4%	2%	1%	0%	0%	10%
<50%	0%	0%	1%	3%	4%	2%	0%	0%	0%	0%	10%
<40%	0%	1%	2%	5%	2%	0%	0%	0%	0%		10%
<30%	1%	3%	4%	2%	0%	0%	0%				9%
<20%	2%	5%	2%	0%	0%	0%					10%
<10%	7%	2%	0%	0%							10%
All	10%	10%	10%	10%	10%	9%	9%	10%	11%	10%	100%

Educational vs. FICO Bureau 2	Rank for FICO Score										
Rank for Educational Score	<10%	<20%	<30%	<40%	<50%	<60%	<70%	<80%	<90%	<100%	All
<100%			0%	0%	0%	0%	1%	2%	3%	4%	11%
<90%			0%	0%	0%	1%	2%	2%	2%	2%	9%
<80%			0%	0%	0%	1%	2%	2%	2%	2%	10%
<70%		0%	0%	0%	1%	2%	3%	2%	2%	1%	11%
<60%		0%	0%	1%	2%	3%	2%	1%	1%	0%	10%
<50%	0%	0%	0%	2%	4%	2%	1%	0%	0%	0%	10%
<40%	0%	1%	3%	4%	2%	0%	0%	0%	0%	0%	10%
<30%	1%	2%	4%	2%	0%	0%	0%	0%			10%
<20%	3%	4%	2%	0%	0%	0%					9%
<10%	6%	3%	0%	0%							10%
All	10%	10%	10%	10%	10%	10%	10%	10%	10%	10%	100%

Appendix Figure 5. (Continued).

Educational vs. FICO Bureau 3	Rank for FICO Score										
Rank for Educational Score	<10%	<20%	<30%	<40%	<50%	<60%	<70%	<80%	<90%	<100%	All
<100%			0%	0%	0%	0%	1%	2%	3%	4%	11%
<90%			0%	0%	0%	1%	2%	3%	3%	3%	12%
<80%		0%		0%	1%	2%	2%	2%	2%	2%	11%
<70%	0%	0%	0%	0%	1%	3%	2%	2%	1%	0%	10%
<60%	0%	0%	0%	1%	3%	3%	1%	1%	0%	0%	9%
<50%	0%	0%	1%	3%	3%	1%	0%	0%	0%	0%	9%
<40%	0%	1%	2%	4%	2%	0%	0%	0%	0%	0%	9%
<30%	1%	2%	4%	2%	0%	0%	0%	0%			10%
<20%	3%	4%	2%	0%	0%	0%					9%
<10%	7%	3%	0%	0%							10%
All	10%	10%	10%	10%	10%	10%	10%	10%	10%	10%	100%

VantageScore vs. Educational Bureau 1	Rank for Educational Score										
Rank for VantageScore	<10%	<20%	<30%	<40%	<50%	<60%	<70%	<80%	<90%	<100%	All
<100%			0%	0%	0%	0%	0%	1%	3%	5%	10%
<90%			0%	0%	0%	0%	1%	2%	4%	3%	10%
<80%		0%	0%	0%	0%	1%	2%	3%	3%	1%	10%
<70%			0%	0%	1%	2%	4%	2%	1%	0%	10%
<60%		0%	0%	1%	2%	3%	2%	1%	1%	0%	10%
<50%	0%	0%	1%	2%	4%	2%	1%	0%	0%	0%	10%
<40%	0%	1%	2%	4%	3%	1%	0%	0%	0%		10%
<30%	1%	2%	4%	2%	0%	0%	0%	0%			10%
<20%	3%	4%	2%	1%	0%	0%	0%				10%
<10%	6%	3%	1%	0%	0%						10%
All	10%	10%	10%	10%	10%	10%	10%	10%	10%	10%	100%

VantageScore vs. Educational Bureau 2	Rank for Educational Score										
Rank for VantageScore	<10%	<20%	<30%	<40%	<50%	<60%	<70%	<80%	<90%	<100%	All
<100%		0%	0%	0%	1%	1%	1%	2%	2%	3%	10%
<90%			0%	0%	0%	1%	2%	2%	2%	3%	10%
<80%			0%	0%	1%	1%	2%	2%	2%	2%	10%
<70%		0%	0%	0%	1%	2%	2%	2%	1%	2%	10%
<60%	0%	0%	0%	1%	2%	2%	2%	1%	1%	1%	10%
<50%	0%	0%	1%	2%	3%	2%	1%	1%	0%	0%	10%
<40%	0%	1%	2%	3%	2%	1%	0%	0%	0%	0%	10%
<30%	1%	2%	4%	2%	1%	0%	0%	0%	0%	0%	10%
<20%	3%	4%	2%	1%	0%	0%	0%				10%
<10%	7%	3%	1%	0%	0%	0%					10%
All	10%	10%	10%	10%	10%	10%	11%	10%	9%	11%	100%

VantageScore vs. Educational Bureau 3	Rank for Educational Score										
Rank for VantageScore	<10%	<20%	<30%	<40%	<50%	<60%	<70%	<80%	<90%	<100%	All
<100%			0%	0%	0%	0%	1%	2%	3%	4%	10%
<90%				0%	0%	0%	1%	2%	3%	3%	10%
<80%			0%	0%	0%	1%	2%	3%	3%	1%	10%
<70%		0%	0%	0%	1%	1%	3%	3%	2%	1%	10%
<60%	0%	0%	0%	1%	2%	3%	3%	1%	1%	0%	10%
<50%	0%	0%	1%	2%	3%	2%	1%	0%	0%	0%	10%
<40%	0%	1%	2%	3%	2%	1%	0%	0%	0%	0%	10%
<30%	1%	3%	4%	2%	1%	0%	0%	0%	0%		10%
<20%	3%	4%	2%	1%	0%	0%	0%			0%	10%
<10%	7%	3%	1%	0%	0%	0%	0%				10%
All	10%	10%	10%	9%	9%	9%	10%	11%	11%	10%	100%

VantageScore vs. FICO Bureau 1	Rank for FICO Score										
Rank for VantageScore	<10%	<20%	<30%	<40%	<50%	<60%	<70%	<80%	<90%	<100%	All
<100%		0%	0%	0%	0%	0%	1%	2%	3%	3%	10%
<90%			0%	0%	0%	1%	1%	2%	3%	4%	10%
<80%		0%		0%	1%	1%	1%	3%	3%	2%	10%
<70%	0%	0%	0%	0%	1%	2%	3%	2%	1%	1%	10%
<60%	0%	0%	0%	1%	2%	3%	3%	1%	0%	0%	10%
<50%	0%	0%	1%	3%	3%	2%	1%	0%	0%	0%	10%
<40%	0%	1%	2%	4%	2%	1%	0%	0%	0%	0%	10%
<30%	1%	3%	3%	2%	0%	0%	0%	0%		0%	10%
<20%	3%	3%	2%	0%	0%	0%	0%	0%			9%
<10%	6%	3%	1%	0%	0%						10%
All	10%	10%	10%	10%	10%	9%	9%	10%	11%	10%	100%

VantageScore vs. FICO Bureau 2	Rank for FICO Score										
Rank for VantageScore	<10%	<20%	<30%	<40%	<50%	<60%	<70%	<80%	<90%	<100%	All
<100%		0%	0%	0%	1%	1%	2%	2%	2%	2%	10%
<90%		0%	0%	0%	1%	1%	2%	2%	2%	2%	10%
<80%		0%		0%	1%	1%	2%	2%	2%	3%	10%
<70%		0%	0%	0%	1%	1%	2%	2%	2%	2%	10%
<60%	0%	0%	0%	1%	2%	2%	2%	2%	1%	1%	10%
<50%	0%	0%	1%	2%	3%	2%	1%	1%	0%	0%	10%
<40%	0%	1%	2%	3%	2%	1%	0%	0%	0%	0%	10%
<30%	1%	2%	4%	2%	1%	0%	0%	0%	0	0%	10%
<20%	3%	4%	2%	0%	0%	0%					9%
<10%	7%	3%	0%	0%	0%	0					10%
All	10%	10%	10%	10%	10%	10%	10%	10%	10%	10%	100%

VantageScore vs. FICO Bureau 3	Rank for FICO Score										
Rank for VantageScore	<10%	<20%	<30%	<40%	<50%	<60%	<70%	<80%	<90%	<100%	All
<100%		0%	0%	0%	0%	0%	1%	2%	3%	4%	11%
<90%			0%	0%	0%	1%	1%	2%	3%	3%	11%
<80%		0%		0%	1%	1%	2%	2%	3%	2%	11%
<70%	0%	0%	0%	0%	1%	2%	3%	2%	1%	1%	11%
<60%	0%	0%	0%	1%	3%	3%	2%	1%	0%	0%	10%
<50%	0%	0%	1%	3%	3%	2%	1%	0%	0%	0%	10%
<40%	0%	1%	3%	3%	2%	1%	0%	0%	0%	0%	9%
<30%	1%	3%	4%	2%	0%	0%	0%	0%			9%
<20%	3%	4%	2%	0%	0%	0%	0%	0%	0		9%
<10%	6%	3%	1%	0%	0%						10%
All	10%	10%	10%	10%	10%	10%	10%	10%	10%	10%	100%

Appendix Figure 5. Decile Comparisons.

Educational vs. FICO Bureau 1		Cumulative
Decile match (green)	42% (75,592)	42% (75,592)
Adjacent deciles (light green)	43% (76,813)	85% (152,405)
Two deciles off (yellow)	11% (20,436)	97% (172,841)
Three or more deciles off (red)	3% (5,736)	100% (178,577)
Total	100% (178,577)	100% (178,577)

Educational vs. Vantage Bureau 1		Cumulative
Decile match (green)	42% (76,435)	42% (76,435)
Adjacent deciles (light green)	44% (81,275)	86% (157,710)
Two deciles off (yellow)	11% (20,472)	97% (178,182)
Three or more deciles off (red)	3% (5,669)	100% (183,851)
Total	100% (183,851)	100% (183,851)

Appendix Figure 6. (Continued).

FICO vs. Vantage Bureau 1		Cumulative
Decile match (green)	34% (60,596)	34% (60,596)
Adjacent deciles (light green)	44% (78,388)	78% (138,984)
Two deciles off (yellow)	16% (28,007)	94% (166,991)
Three or more deciles off (red)	6% (10,718)	100% (177,709)
Total	100% (177,709)	100% (177,709)

Educational vs. FICO Bureau 2		Cumulative
Decile match (green)	36% (71,108)	36% (71,108)
Adjacent deciles (light green)	42% (83,061)	78% (154,169)
Two deciles off (yellow)	15% (29,397)	94% (183,566)
Three or more deciles off (red)	6% (11,932)	100% (195,498)
Total	100% (195,498)	100% (195,498)

FICO vs. Vantage Bureau 2		Cumulative
Decile match (green)	30% (58,889)	30% (58,889)
Adjacent deciles (light green)	38% (73,181)	68% (132,070)
Two deciles off (yellow)	19% (37,182)	87% (169,252)
Three or more deciles off (red)	13% (25,706)	100% (194,958)
Total	100% (194,958)	100% (194,598)

Educational vs. Vantage Bureau 2		Cumulative
Decile match (green)	31% (62,289)	31% (62,3289)
Adjacent deciles (light green)	39% (77,659)	70% (139,948)
Two deciles off (yellow)	18% (34,678)	88% (174,626)
Three or more deciles off (red)	12% (23,181)	100% (197,807)
Total	100% (197,807)	100% (197,807)

Educational vs. FICO Bureau 3		Cumulative
Decile match (green)	38% (63,327)	38% (63,327)
Adjacent deciles (light green)	42% (70,340)	80% (133,667)
Two deciles off (yellow)	15% (24,413)	95% (158,080)
Three or more deciles off (red)	5% (8,364)	100% (166,444)
Total	100% (166,444)	100% (166,444)

Educational vs. Vantage Bureau 3		Cumulative
Decile match (green)	36% (62,314)	36% (62,314)
Adjacent deciles (light green)	43% (74,612)	78% (136,926)
Two deciles off (yellow)	16% (28,314)	94% (163,240)
Three or more deciles off (red)	6% (10,180)	100% (175,420)
Total	100% (175,420)	100% (175,420)

FICO vs. Vantage Bureau 3		Cumulative
Decile match (green)	35% (57,252)	35% (57,252)
Adjacent deciles (light green)	42% (69,584)	77% (126,836)
Two deciles off (yellow)	17% (27,863)	93% (154,699)
Three or more deciles off (red)	7% (10,778)	100% (165,477)
Total	100% (165,477)	100% (165,477)

Appendix Figure 6. Decile Analysis.

Educational vs. FICO Bureau 1	FICO Score				
Educational Score	< 620	620 - 680	680 - 740	> 740	All
>740	0%	0%	4%	39%	44%
680 - 740	0%	3%	9%	3%	15%
620 - 680	3%	9%	3%	0%	15%
< 620	23%	3%	0%	0%	26%
All	27%	15%	16%	42%	100%

Educational vs. VantageScore Bureau 1	Educational Score				
Rank for VantageScore	< 620	620 - 680	680 - 740	> 740	All
Over 55%	0%	0%	5%	40%	45%
< 55%	1%	5%	8%	3%	17%
< 38%	4%	7%	2%	0%	13%
< 25%	22%	3%	0%	0%	25%
All	27%	15%	16%	43%	100%

FICO vs. VantageScore Bureau 1	FICO Score				
Rank for VantageScore	< 620	620 - 680	680 - 740	> 740	All
Over 55%	0%	1%	7%	39%	47%
< 55%	1%	5%	7%	4%	17%
< 38%	4%	6%	2%	0%	13%
< 25%	21%	2%	0%	0%	24%
All	27%	15%	16%	43%	100%

Educational vs. FICO Bureau 2	FICO Score				
Educational Score	< 620	620 - 680	680 - 740	> 740	All
>740	0%	0%	5%	51%	56%
680 - 740	0%	3%	9%	3%	16%
620 - 680	3%	5%	2%	0%	10%
< 620	15%	3%	0%	0%	18%
All	18%	12%	16%	54%	100%

Educational vs. VantageScore Bureau 2	Educational Score				
Rank for VantageScore	< 620	620 - 680	680 - 740	> 740	All
Over 55%	0%	0%	3%	42%	45%
< 55%	0%	1%	5%	11%	17%
< 38%	1%	4%	6%	2%	13%
< 25%	17%	5%	2%	0%	25%
All	19%	11%	16%	56%	100%

Appendix Figure 7. (Continued).

FICO vs. VantageScore Bureau 2	FICO Score				
Rank for VantageScore	< 620	620 - 680	680 - 740	> 740	All
Over 55%	0%	0%	3%	42%	46%
< 55%	0%	1%	5%	10%	17%
< 38%	1%	4%	6%	2%	13%
< 25%	16%	6%	2%	0%	24%
All	18%	12%	16%	54%	100%

Educational vs. FICO Bureau 3	FICO Score				
Educational Score	< 620	620 - 680	680 - 740	> 740	All
>740	0%	0%	3%	35%	38%
680 - 740	0%	3%	10%	8%	22%
620 - 680	3%	8%	3%	0%	15%
< 620	23%	3%	0%	0%	26%
All	26%	14%	17%	46%	100%

Educational vs. VantageScore Bureau 3	Educational Score				
Rank for VantageScore	< 620	620 - 680	680 - 740	> 740	All
Over 55%	0%	1%	10%	34%	45%
< 55%	1%	5%	9%	2%	17%
< 38%	4%	6%	3%	0%	13%
< 25%	22%	3%	0%	0%	25%
All	27%	15%	22%	36%	100%

FICO vs. VantageScore Bureau 3	FICO Score				
Rank for VantageScore	< 620	620 - 680	680 - 740	> 740	All
Over 55%	0%	1%	7%	40%	48%
< 55%	1%	5%	7%	4%	17%
< 38%	4%	6%	2%	0%	12%
< 25%	21%	2%	0%	0%	23%
All	27%	14%	17%	47%	100%

Appendix Figure 7. Score Range Comparisons.

FICO vs. Educational Bureau 1		Cumulative
Same score category (green)	80% (142,493)	80% (142,493)
One category off (yellow)	19% (34,631)	99% (177,124)
More than one category off (red)	1% (1,454)	100% (178,578)
Total	100% (178,578)	100% (178,578)

Educational vs. Vantage Bureau 1		Cumulative
Same score category (green)	77% (141,916)	77% (141,916)
One category off (yellow)	22% (39,763)	99% (181,679)
More than one category off (red)	1% (2,172)	100% (183,851)
Total	100% (183,851)	100% (183,851)

FICO vs. Vantage Bureau 1		Cumulative
Same score category (green)	73% (129,858)	73% (129,858)
One category off (yellow)	24% (42,941)	97% (172,799)
More than one category off (red)	3% (4,910)	100% (177,709)
Total	100% (177,709)	100% (177,709)

FICO vs. Educational Bureau 2		Cumulative
Same score category (green)	80% (155,618)	80% (155,618)
One category off (yellow)	20% (38,388)	99% (194,006)
More than one category off (red)	1% (1,492)	100% (195,498)
Total	100% (195,498)	100% (195,498)

Educational vs. Vantage Bureau 2		Cumulative
Same score category (green)	68% (135,421)	68% (135,421)
One category off (yellow)	27% (52,707)	95% (188,128)
More than one category off (red)	5% (9,679)	100% (197,807)
Total	100% (197,807)	100% (197,807)

FICO vs. Vantage Bureau 2		Cumulative
Same score category (green)	68% (86,706)	68% (86,706)
One category off (yellow)	28% (54,126)	96% (140,832)
More than one category off (red)	4% (7,949)	100% (194,958)
Total	100% (194,958)	100% (194,958)

FICO vs. Educational Bureau 3		Cumulative
Same score category (green)	75% (125,636)	75% (125,636)
One category off (yellow)	23% (38,961)	98% (164,597)
More than one category off (red)	1% (1,847)	100% (166,444)
Total	100% (166,444)	100% (166,444)

Educational vs. Vantage Bureau 3		Cumulative
Same score category (green)	71% (124,430)	71% (124,430)
One category off (yellow)	26% (46,433)	97% (170,863)
More than one category off (red)	3% (4,557)	100% (175,420)
Total	100% (175,420)	100% (175,420)

FICO vs. Vantage Bureau 3		Cumulative
Same score category (green)	74% (121,776)	74% (121,776)
One category off (yellow)	24% (39,308)	97% (161,084)
More than one category off (red)	3% (4,393)	100% (165,477)
Total	100% (165,477)	100% (165,477)

Appendix Figure 8. Score Range Analysis.

Bureau 1	Educational Median	FICO Median	Vantage Median	Difference	Educational Median	FICO Median	Vantage Median	Difference
	Younger				Older			
Educational vs. FICO	35	35	-	0	74	74	-	0
Educational vs. Vantage	35	-	31	4	74	-	72	2
FICO vs. Vantage	-	35	32	-3	-	74	73	-1
	Customers in LMI Areas				Customers in Non-LMI Areas			
Educational vs. FICO	36	34	-	2	54	52	-	2
Educational vs. Vantage	35	-	35	0	53	-	53	0
FICO vs. Vantage	-	34	36	2	-	52	54	2
	Majority Minority Areas				Low Minority Areas			
Educational vs. FICO	36	34	-	2	54	52	-	2
Educational vs. Vantage	35	-	35	0	53	-	53	0
FICO vs. Vantage	-	34	37	3	-	53	55	2

Bureau 2	Educational Median	FICO Median	Vantage Median	Difference	Educational Median	FICO Median	Vantage Median	Difference
	Younger				Older			
Educational vs. FICO					64	66	-	-2
Educational vs. Vantage					63	-	61	2
FICO vs. Vantage					-	66	61	-5
	Customers in LMI Areas				Customers in Non-LMI Areas			
Educational vs. FICO	37	36	-	1	52	51	-	1
Educational vs. Vantage	36	-	36	0	52	-	52	0
FICO vs. Vantage	-	37	37	0	-	52	52	0
	Majority Minority Areas				Low Minority Areas			
Educational vs. FICO	35	34	-	1	53	52	-	1
Educational vs. Vantage	34	-	34	0	53	-	52	1
FICO vs. Vantage	-	34	35	1	-	52	52	0

Bureau 3	Educational Median	FICO Median	Vantage Median	Difference	Educational Median	FICO Median	Vantage Median	Difference
	Younger				Older			
Educational vs. FICO	35	34	-	1	74	74	-	0
Educational vs. Vantage	35	-	31	4	73	-	70	3
FICO vs. Vantage	-	34	32	-2	-	74	71	-3
	Customers in LMI Areas				Customers in Non-LMI Areas			
Educational vs. FICO	36	34	-	2	56	52	-	4
Educational vs. Vantage	34	-	34	0	55	-	53	2
FICO vs. Vantage	-	34	37	3	-	52	55	3
	Majority Minority Areas				Low Minority Areas			
Educational vs. FICO	36	34	-	2	57	52	-	5
Educational vs. Vantage	34	-	34	0	55	-	53	2
FICO vs. Vantage	-	34	37	3	-	52	56	4

Appendix Figure 9. Median Score Comparisons.

Bureau 1	Younger		Older
Educational vs. FICO	0.92	>	0.90
Educational vs. Vantage	0.91	>	0.90
FICO vs. Vantage	0.89	>	0.85
	Customers in LMI Areas		Customers in Non-LMI Areas
Educational vs. FICO	0.94	>	0.93
Educational vs. Vantage	0.93	~	0.93
FICO vs. Vantage	0.91	>	0.90
	Majority Minority Areas		Low Minority Areas
Educational vs. FICO	0.94	>	0.93
Educational vs. Vantage	0.93	~	0.93
FICO vs. Vantage	0.90	~	0.90

Bureau 2	Younger		Older
Educational vs. FICO			0.88
Educational vs. Vantage			0.80
FICO vs. Vantage			0.78
	Customers in LMI Areas		Customers in Non-LMI Areas
Educational vs. FICO	0.92	>	0.90
Educational vs. Vantage	0.93	~	0.93
FICO vs. Vantage	0.87	>	0.83
	Majority Minority Areas		Low Minority Areas
Educational vs. FICO	0.92	<	0.93
Educational vs. Vantage	0.93	>	0.90
FICO vs. Vantage	0.86	>	0.83

Bureau 3	Younger		Older
Educational vs. FICO	0.90	>	0.87
Educational vs. Vantage	0.87	~	0.87
FICO vs. Vantage	0.89	>	0.84
	Customers in LMI Areas		Customers in Non-LMI Areas
Educational vs. FICO	0.93	>	0.91
Educational vs. Vantage	0.91	>	0.90
FICO vs. Vantage	0.91	>	0.89
	Majority Minority Areas		Low Minority Areas
Educational vs. FICO	0.92	>	0.91
Educational vs. Vantage	0.91	>	0.90
FICO vs. Vantage	0.90	>	0.89

Appendix Figure 10. Median Score Correlations.

End Notes

[1] Dodd-Frank Wall Street Reform and Consumer Protection Act, Pub. L. 111-203, sec. 1078, 124 Stat. 1376, 2076 (enacted July 21, 2010).

[2] Consumer Financial Protection Bureau, "The Impact of Differences between Consumer and Creditor-Purchased Credit Scores," (July 19, 2011).

[3] See, e.g., Equifax, Things You Should Know… (online at https://help.equifax.com/app/answers/detail/a_id/386/~/things-you- should-know...) ("The Equifax Credit Score … is intended for your own educational use. There are numerous credit scores and models available in the marketplace and lenders may use a different score when evaluating your creditworthiness."); Experian, online at www.experian.com ("Experian Credit Score indicates your relative credit risk level for educational purposes and is not the score used by lenders.")

[4] See Equifax product information online, at: https://help.equifax.com/app/answers/detail/a_id/386/~/things-you- should-know...

[5] Experian, FAQ: What is a PLUS Score (online at http://www.nationalscore.com/FAQ.aspx).

[6] CreditKarma, online at http://www.creditkarma.com/preview/score/. This score, unlike the others, is specifically designed to predict risk on new accounts, rather than new and existing accounts.

[7] A lender must provide consumers a credit score if (1) the lender provided credit on material terms that are materially less favorable than the most favorable material terms available to a substantial proportion of consumers from or through that lender based in whole or in part on a consumer report, (2) the consumer applies for a mortgage loan and the mortgage lender uses credit scores, or (3) when the lender takes adverse action against the consumer based in whole or in part on information in a consumer report. See Consumer Financial Protection Bureau, "The Impact of Differences between Consumer and Creditor- Purchased Credit Scores," at 12 (July 19, 2011).

[8] Fannie Mae Selling Guide Announcement 09-29, September 22, 2009, page 2.

[9] The Bureau received only the information described in the body of the report. The Bureau did not receive name, Social Security Number, address information beyond ZIP code, or other identifying information.

[10] Credit scores sold to predict payment behavior for a wide range of products are typically called "generic" scores. When scores are designed more specifically to predict behavior for one type of credit, such as automobile loans or credit cards, they are referred to as "industry" scores. The most specific scores, typically used by individual lenders and calculated from a combination of bureau and other information, are called "custom" scores.

[11] FICO Auto scores had a correlation of 0.99, 0.95, and 0.98 for bureaus 1, 2 and 3 respectively with a generic FICO score. FICO Bank Card scores had a correlation of 0.99, 0.99, and 0.99 for bureaus 1, 2, and 3 respectively with generic FICO scores.

[12] Because older consumers tend to have higher credit scores, the median credit score for this CRA is higher than that of the other two CRAs. Because the correlations across scoring models are lower for consumers with higher credit scores the correlations across scores are lower at this CRA. The results are fully consistent with the different age distribution in this CRA's sample, and therefore we do not believe there are substantial differences in the correlations across models at this CRA but rather that these differences are the result of the sampling differences.

[13] Default risk derived from report of odds ratio of any 90 day delinquency or any derogatory note in trade lines from FICO Score Trend Validation Chart. Default risk was taken as 1/(1+ odds ratio).

[14] Deciles were defined for each score for all consumers that had that score. Rows and columns of the tables do not always add up to exactly 10% because of missing scores. Some consumers in the sample were missing one or more scores, and in each pairwise comparison

of the scores the distribution of missing values was not even across all deciles; some deciles had slightly more or slightly less than 10% when missing scores were removed from the table. For example at one bureau, VantageScore was missing on 0.81% of the sample when an educational score was reported. Conversely, the educational score was missing on 0.19% of the sample when VantageScore was reported. FICO scores were missing on 3.44% of the sample when the educational score was provided. Conversely, the educational score was missing on 4.46% of the sample when FICO scores were provided. FICO scores were missing on 3.26% of the sample when VantageScore was provided, and VantageScores were missing on 4.90% of the sample when FICO was provided.

[15] Each comparison across scoring models is for consumers with scores from both models, so the sample used varies across comparisons. This approach was used to ensure that differences across scoring models are driven entirely by differences in the models, and not differences in the sample that has each score. This is why the median score for a given group – such as median VantageScore for young consumers – varies across comparisons.

[16] Younger consumers were defined as those with ages from 18 to 25. The three CRAs did not have consumers below age 18.

[17] Older consumers were defined as those age 62 or more.

[18] Zip codes were matched to 2000 Census ZCTA data and classified into low, moderate, middle and upper income areas. Low and moderate income areas have less than 80 percent of median household income.

[19] High minority population was defined as an area with 50% or more minorities.

[20] Report to Congress on Credit Scoring and its Effects on the Availability and Affordability of Credit, Board of Governors of the Federal Reserve System (August 2007).

[21] New York Times, "Why you have 49 different FICO Scores (online at http://bucks.blogs).

[22] See http://www.myfico.com/crediteducation/creditinquiries.aspx.

[23] CFPB conversation with Barrett Burns, CEO, VantageScore®, August 28, 2012.

INDEX

N

O

P

R

S

T

U

V

W